Hugh Mackay is an Australian social researcher and bestselling author. He has a master's degree in moral philosophy and was one of the founders of the St James Ethics Centre.

In recognition of his pioneering work in social research, he has been awarded honorary doctorates by Charles Sturt, Macquarie, New South Wales, Western Sydney and Wollongong universities. He was elected a Fellow of the Australian Psychological Society in 1984 and received the University of Sydney Alumni Award for achievement in community service in 2004. He was appointed an Officer of the Order of Australia in 2015.

Also by Hugh Mackay

NON-FICTION

Reinventing Australia
Why Don't People Listen?
(also published as *The Good Listener*)
Generations
Turning Point
Media Mania
Advance Australia . . . Where?
What Makes Us Tick
The Good Life
The Art of Belonging
Beyond Belief
Australia Reimagined

FICTION

Little Lies
House Guest
The Spin
Winter Close
Ways of Escape
Infidelity
Selling the Dream

RIGHT & WRONG

How to decide for yourself, make wiser moral choices and build a better society

HUGH MACKAY

hachette
AUSTRALIA

Extract from *A Short Treatise on the Great Virtues* by André Comte-Sponville published by William Heinemann, used by permission of The Random House Group Limited. Extract from *Gravity and Grace* by Simone Weil published by Routledge, used by permission of Thomson Publishing Services. Extract from *When All You've Ever Wanted Isn't Enough* by Harold Kushner published by Pan Books, used by permission of Pan Macmillan Ltd, UK. Extracts from *An Intimate History of Humanity* by Theodore Zeldin published by Sinclair-Stevenson, used by permission of The Random House Group Limited. Extracts from articles by Pamela Bone in the *Age* and Geoff Kitney in the *Sydney Morning Herald* used by permission of the authors.

Every effort has been made to acknowledge and contact the owners of copyright for permission to reproduce material which falls under the *Copyright Act 1968*. Any copyright owners who have inadvertently been omitted from acknowledgements and credits should contact the publisher and omissions will be rectified in subsequent editions.

The italicised and indented paragraphs in the text are based on verbatim quotations from participants in Hugh Mackay's social research projects.

 hachette
AUSTRALIA

First published in Australia and New Zealand in 2004
by Hodder Australia
(an imprint of Hachette Australia Pty Limited)
Level 17, 207 Kent Street, Sydney NSW 2000
www.hachette.com.au

This edition published in 2019

10 9 8 7 6 5 4 3 2 1

NATIONAL LIBRARY OF AUSTRALIA

A catalogue record for this book is available from the National Library of Australia

ISBN: 978 0 7336 4165 7 (paperback)

Cover design by Blue Cork
Author photograph by Lorrie Graham
Text design by Bookhouse, Sydney
Typeset in 11/15.8 pt Adobe Caslon by Bookhouse, Sydney
Printed and bound in Australia by McPherson's Printing Group

MIX
Paper from responsible sources
FSC
www.fsc.org
FSC® C001695

The paper this book is printed on is certified against the Forest Stewardship Council® Standards. McPherson's Printing Group holds FSC® chain of custody certification SA-COC-005379. FSC® promotes environmentally responsible, socially beneficial and economically viable management of the world's forests.

To my children:
Stephen, Greg, Kirsty,
David & James

**We don't see things as they are;
we see things as we are.**

—ANAÏS NIN

Contents

The moral minefields of power and wealth

In the fourteen years since the second edition of *Right & Wrong* was published, Australia has had seven prime ministers and none of those who have held office since 2007 has survived a full term of government. That may tell you something about the impatience of the greed for power and, in the case of some deposed leaders, the urgency of the lust for revenge. It may also remind you that the seeking or wielding of power—political and otherwise—can do strange things to people and institutions, often bringing out the worst in them and sometimes even corrupting them. That's why power is a moral minefield.

And so is wealth. In the Preface to the second edition, I raised these three questions: 'Does the emergence of a wealth class in Australia spell the end of the egalitarian dream? Are class divisions becoming institutionalised? Is the gap between the top and bottom of the economic heap already so great that it may never be closed (and do we even want to close it)?' Since then, the income-inequality gap has widened even further, underemployment and job insecurity look like becoming permanent features of the labour market, and about two million Australians (including 800,000 children) are still living in poverty, while the wealthy have been finding ever more creative ways of protecting and extending their wealth.

These are all moral issues, because they relate to our willingness—as individuals and as a society—to accept responsibility for each other's wellbeing.

But let's return to politics . . .

Power and sex

In February 2018, Malcolm Turnbull strode to the prime ministerial lectern outside his office and delivered a stern rebuke to his then-deputy, Barnaby Joyce, over Mr Joyce's sexual conduct. More broadly, Mr Turnbull declared that no government minister should ever have sexual relations with a member of their staff, as a matter of principle.

The then-PM's lecture was triggered by the fact that aspects of Barnaby Joyce's private life had become public knowledge and a series of salacious revelations were distracting the government. If its purpose was to make the deputy prime minister's position untenable then, to the extent that it achieved that end, it could be regarded as a successful political tactic (though within six months, the Turnbull prime ministership itself was at an end and Mr Joyce's political rehabilitation had begun).

Beautiful romances and, indeed, lifelong marriages can begin in the workplace. But the inherent risk of a professional conflict of interest always lurks, as does the possibility that a power imbalance might add a layer of complexity to the relationship that might not always be apparent to the participants themselves. Some of the media commentary at the time of the Joyce affair implied that people engaging in a sexual relationship with a high-status person might turn out to have been mere pawns in a power game, being flattered or perhaps even overawed by the attentions of a person of such superior rank and status as a government minister. ('VIP' is a corrosive concept, in any context, but it does reflect the aura of power that tends to develop around some people whose status derives from their position or wealth, or merely from their fame.)

At its ugliest and most grotesque, of course, a power imbalance can lead to the flagrant sexual exploitation and abuse of people who are vulnerable to the influence of the abuser. Starting with revelations about Hollywood producer Harvey Weinstein, the #MeToo movement has spread across the world, encouraging people (mainly women) to name and shame those (mainly men) in positions of power who have abused that power by making predatory sexual advances, or by suggesting that promotion and preferment might follow from sexual acquiescence.

Mr Turnbull's statement on the subject of ministerial sexual conduct was consistent with many utterances made by—or about—public figures that seem to imply that sexual impropriety is a special case; that their deviation from an accepted norm of sexual behaviour is particularly disgraceful in a way that, for example, their deviation from a norm of financial probity or other aspects of human propriety (loyalty, fidelity, truth-telling) are not. Or perhaps even that sexual misconduct raises broader questions about a public figure's integrity.

Perhaps sexual morality *is* perceived differently, simply because our sexual mores spring from ancient and primitive rules and customs related to parenthood, inheritance, ownership of property, tribal customs, family ties, etc. In the modern world, those foundations have shifted, but the tendency to moralise about sex persists, as if straying from sexual norms is a *particularly* corrupt form of behaviour, perhaps because it does relate to that most basic of human activities: the procreation of the species. (And there is a sense in which we are all affected by the instability of marriage: we have become a high-divorce society, which means our attitudes to the institution of marriage have inevitably changed and many people regret that—while others celebrate it as a sign that we are taking marriage more, not less, seriously.)

Even when—as in Mr Joyce's case—no laws have been broken and, some would argue, it's nobody's business but those directly involved, many people do feel entitled both to gossip and to pontificate about other people's sex lives. They do this without restraint, compassion, or respect for the privacy of the individuals concerned and, often, without a hint of self-consciousness about the non-sexual moral lapses and ambiguities in their own life.

Yet the inevitable price to be paid for moralising about others' behaviour is that attention will be focused on the moral aspects of your own behaviour. For example, in the Turnbull/Joyce context, how should Mr Joyce's sexual behaviour be ranked, on some theoretical scale of unworthiness, compared with, say, Mr Turnbull's disloyalty to the two Liberal Party leaders he deposed—Brendan Nelson and Tony Abbott? More generally, we could ask whether the sexual misconduct of any minister is worse than, say, a minister bullying or intimidating a colleague or, indeed, a member of the public, telling lies, breaking promises to the electorate, or retreating from a previously declared matter of principle. And surely, on any scale of dubious morality, sexual conduct would rank far below the despatching of Australian troops to participate in the 2003 invasion of Iraq—a war not sanctioned by the United Nations and, indeed, declared illegal by Kofi Annan, the UN Secretary General at the time.

What about financial morality?

Disrupted sexual relationships are often messy—especially when children are involved—but they rarely have any significant impact on anyone beyond a small circle of family and friends. To that extent, their moral implications are very limited. There is no consequence for the wider society (except that most people are still attracted to the ideal of stable marriages as one contributor to a stable society, so every fractured marriage is a challenge to that ideal).

Compare that to the moral implications of wealthy people parking huge sums of money in offshore bank accounts, creating family trusts, or taking any other steps to avoid ('minimise' is the polite word) paying income tax. All such steps deprive the public purse of considerable sums of money: on any moral scale, the implications for the wellbeing of others are far greater than those that arise from private sexual conduct.

The offshore account strategy is particularly egregious because it is such a flagrant means of avoiding income tax contributions to the economy of your home country. Some wealthy people are quite untroubled by this concept: they may justify their avoidance of tax responsibility by pointing to their personal philanthropy, for instance, as if their great wealth entitles them to decide how any surplus money should be directed (for example, to a favourite charity), rather than it going, via taxation, to help with the implementation of government policies on health, education, welfare or infrastructure spending.

There's nothing illegal in any of these tax-minimisation strategies, of course, just as there is nothing illegal about having an affair. But if morality is about the way we treat each other, and our willingness to accept responsibility for each other's wellbeing, then minimising your tax obligations *in Australia* by transferring funds to other jurisdictions raises some lively moral issues that range far more widely than a bit of sexual hanky-panky—or even a bit of serious, loving sex—in a ministerial office or elsewhere. Even more than home-based tax minimisation strategies, offshore accounts are a way of saying to your fellow Australians, 'I don't take you seriously enough to contribute my fair share to the nation's coffers.'

Wealth, particularly wealth amassed quickly, is a moral minefield, partly because it tends to create a sense of entitlement among the wealthy—'I'm special . . . look how rich I am!'—and partly because it encourages an unattractive attitude of disdain towards the less wealthy, let alone the poor. I once heard an eminent (and very wealthy) company director say of a distinguished Australian who was being considered for appointment to the board of governors of a private institution, 'He hasn't made any money,' as if that were all that needed to be said to terminate the person's candidacy.

The two faces of ambition

A fundamental principle of morality is breached whenever our ambition for power or wealth leads us to place our own interests above the wellbeing of those who are likely to be affected by our actions.

Ambition is a tricky concept. We laud it, as if it's a kind of turbocharger that gets us motivated and drives us to achieve more than we otherwise might. 'They lacked ambition' is generally meant as criticism. Yet the line between ambition and greed is a very blurry one when ambition is about the quest for personal power, status or wealth.

We hear of politicians, for example, who 'always wanted to be prime minister' ever since they were in school: indeed, former Liberal senator Amanda Vanstone once said that she'd never known any prime minister who *didn't* aspire to that office from a very early age, suggesting that if you want to fight your way through the ranks to achieve that office, you would need to be driven by a lifelong ambition.

That may be so, but the question remains: what is the ambition *for*? If the ambition is merely to *be* prime minister, then that smacks of greed for power and status—a motive as ugly as any other form of greed. Such a person might well achieve the goal they aspire to, since that kind of *personal* ambition would likely be linked to a certain ruthlessness and a capacity for making self-serving deals on the way to the top. And yet, if becoming prime minister is your ambition, the danger is that your ambition will have been satisfied by the mere achievement of that office. What then?

Single-minded ambition for 'the top job' in any field is dangerous, simply because it exists in a moral vacuum. It's not about what I might be able to achieve for those I lead if I were to get that job; it's about me getting that job. Period. As another prominent company director once said to me, in all seriousness: 'It's no fun being anything but chairman.'

Contrast the ambition to be 'top' or 'to win' with the ambition to create a more harmonious or equitable society; the ambition to eradicate poverty; the ambition to transition your country to a clean-energy future; the ambition to improve disadvantaged children's access to a word-class public education system; the ambition to ensure true gender equality. Those ambitions might well drive a person to seek high office as a means of achieving those ends, rather than simply to say, 'Hey look at me! I made it!'

If the ambition is simply to be the boss, where will the policy agenda come from? Where the vision? Where the convictions? Where the drive to use high office to bring about a better society? Where the noble impulses towards public service we yearn to see in our leaders in politics, business, academia, the professions or any other aspect of human endeavour?

Ambition—like power and wealth—is a moral minefield. Where it is self-indulgent, it is bound to explode, in the end, for lack of a higher purpose. Where it is directed towards the betterment of society, the risk of self-destruction is less serious, though the risk of being corrupted by power always lurks, even among those who initially seek it only as an instrument for doing good.

The collapse of trust in institutions

At a time when many people feel as if they are losing their moral bearings (partly because the moral landscape itself is becoming more confusing), there is a disconcerting erosion of trust in the moral authority of many of the institutions we have traditionally looked to for leadership. Every society needs its institutions: we create them to preserve the ideals and traditions that express a society's values, and to create a framework for us to do things co-operatively and collectively that we can't do individually (such as run a legal, financial or education system, or a democracy). Institutions are part of who we are; they provide a stable context for our way of life; they exist to serve us.

When we sense that institutions have turned their focus inward and become more concerned with the preservation of their own wealth and power than with serving the common good, we naturally become wary, cynical and disillusioned. And that is a pretty good description of current attitudes to institutions as varied as federal politics, the churches, banks (and big business more generally), the mass media, trade unions, professional sport and even some universities. The 2017 global Edelman Trust Barometer reported its biggest-ever drop in trust in governments, business, media and NGOs, with the drop in Australia among the largest. It also reported that 59 per cent of Australians feel 'the system is failing'.

A 2017 survey conducted by Ipsos reported that 70 per cent of Australians believe the nation 'needs a strong leader to take the country back from the rich and powerful', 68 per cent believe 'the economy is rigged to the advantage of the rich and powerful' and 61 per cent believe traditional parties and politicians 'don't care about people like me'. All of that is consistent with the idea that institutions are bound to lose the trust and respect of a society when they are perceived as turning their focus away from the common good towards the preservation of their own power and the nurturing of their own power base.

Australia's 2017–18 Royal Commission into Institutional Responses to Child Sexual Abuse shocked the nation and further confirmed the growing suspicion that the Roman Catholic Church, like so many other institutions, had been corrupted by its own power. (Other religious and non-religious institutions were also implicated in the abuse of children, but the numbers were highest in the Catholic Church.) There was a lot of talk about the 'culture' of the institution and plenty of evidence to suggest that culture had become self-serving to the extent that some people holding high office in the church were prepared to turn a blind eye (or, worse, to offer protection) to priests who had committed criminal sexual offences against children. The problem was not with the religion; the problem was with the abusers' sense of their own power and the protective power of the institution itself—power that, ironically, depended on the sustained trust of the faithful.

When such scandals emerge, it is usually the perpetrators and those who knowingly protect them who are exposed to public shame and criminal charges. But if the problem lies in the culture of the organisation, then those in ultimate authority ought also to be held to account. Institutionally— whether in religion, politics, banking, business, academia or sport—the rot almost always sets in at the top. And if it doesn't start there, by the setting of a tone that condones misconduct, then it certainly stops there. US President Harry Truman famously had a sign on his desk that read: 'The buck stops here.' And 'here'—the very top—is where the buck always stops. (Other cultures seem to grasp this more clearly than we do.)

It's become a truism of power that, in the words of the English Catholic historian, politician and writer Lord Acton, 'Power tends to corrupt and absolute power corrupts absolutely.' Based on his close, personal observations of the operation of power and influence in high places, he added, 'Great men are almost always bad men,' by which he meant that the exercise of authority and influence can have a corrosive effect on a person's moral integrity. The implication was not that all who *seek* power and authority are 'bad', but that the experience of greatness tends to corrupt. (Notice he said that power *tends* to corrupt and that great men are *almost* always bad men—it was not a universal observation.)

In Australia, a second royal commission—this time into misconduct in the banking, superannuation and financial services industry—further fuelled the disillusionment with institutions and reinforced the growing conviction that power tends to corrupt institutions just as it does individuals, and for essentially the same reasons.

Again, there was much talk of 'the culture' of the banks and other financial organisations, notably AMP. Again, there was a growing realisation that although some employees of these organisations had indeed been guilty of 'misconduct' (to put it mildly) ranging from exploitation of customers to manipulation of markets, questions about culture needed to be directed at the very top of these organisations—to their CEOs and boards.

When AMP's serious misconduct was exposed at the royal commission, the chair and three other directors immediately resigned, and that was widely seen as an appropriate response (as was the 20 per cent pay cut taken by the remaining directors). At the time of writing, however, none of the chairs or other directors of the major banks, who include some of the most experienced, most widely admired and most respected figures in corporate Australia, had been exposed to public scrutiny, though ANZ, CBA and NAB were all facing the prospect of *criminal* charges—two arising from the royal commission and one, ANZ, from an investigation by the Australian Competition and Consumer Commission.

Even before the royal commission began, Federal Court Justice Jayne Jagot had declared in 2017 that the public should be 'shocked, and indeed disgusted' by the behaviour of ANZ and NAB in relation to their manipulation of the bank bill swap rate. But subsequent revelations in the royal commission have created the impression that all the major banks have been guilty of such seriously self-serving misconduct as to justify the term 'corruption'.

Boards and their chairs may argue that it is the CEO who determines the culture of a corporation. But those directors are paid very handsomely for their role in corporate governance and a major part of that role includes the hiring and firing of chief executives. In most cases, board chairs will be in constant contact with their CEOs. So who is ultimately responsible for the 'culture' of a bank or any other large corporation? Everyone who errs must share the blame for bank misconduct but, as with any organisation, it is the governors who are ultimately and inescapably responsible for the culture.

There is nothing inevitable about individuals and institutions being corrupted by their own power, but it's clear that it takes a person of strong moral courage to resist the tug of self-interest—and self-aggrandisement—that comes from the exercise of power, authority and influence. Questions need to be consistently asked by people in such positions, as they address the moral implications of every decision they make: *Is this the right thing to do? Is it in the best interests of all concerned? How would our constituents judge us if they knew the whole truth about what we are doing?*

Another kind of power

The kind of power that corrupts is only one kind of power—the kind derived from a male supremacist heritage and based on a hierarchical view of the world, with some people 'up there' and the rest of us 'down here'. It's about control; about dominance; about superiority and inferiority. It's about winners and losers. And it encourages a hollow elitism and a tendency to be judgmental.

It also encourages bullying and intimidation. From politics to our boardrooms, factories, offices and prisons, via the entertainment industry and all the dark places now being lit up by the #MeToo movement's exposure of gender-based intimidation, people in positions of power and influence too often act as if their status entitles them to intimidate others. Sometimes it's naked and brutal; sometimes it's genteel and discreet. Always it's ugly, inexcusable and wrong. It's corrupt. No one would explicitly condone it, yet it's always been present as a by-product of the traditional power paradigm.

There are other ways of thinking about power that might not eliminate corruption, but would go some way towards reducing its relentless probability. Think, for instance, about the power of co-operation; about the idea that we are all engaged in the same big society-building project. If each of us saw our role in society in those terms, we'd waste less time and energy denigrating, exploiting and belittling (let alone bullying) each other, and acting as if life were a contest in which we had to make every post a winner.

There's a kind of moral purity about the idea of co-operation that is lacking in a rampantly individualistic and highly competitive or adversarial culture. The communitarian spirit is also true to our nature as members of a social species that has always organised itself into communities—herds, tribes, villages, towns, suburbs. All of us depend on such communities for our all-important sense of belonging, our material comfort, our physical and emotional security and even our sense of identity, since 'Who am I?' is a question that can only be sensibly answered in a social context. Co-operation is in our DNA. Of course, we will sometimes compete—on the sporting field, in a commercial marketplace, in the job market—but if we were to commit ourselves to the goal of creating a more co-operative, harmonious culture, our mindset might be healthier, our neuroses less intense, our anxiety levels lower and our lives more satisfying.

There are other kinds of power, closely related to the core concept of co-operation. Think about the power of love; the power of kindness; the power of mutual respect; the power of compassion; the power of forgiveness. It's hard to see how a focus on such versions of power could corrupt us. It's hard to imagine a moral minefield lying in wait for those who seek no power over others, but only to work co-operatively and collaboratively in the common task of making the world a better place.

Hopelessly idealistic? Before you allow yourself such an easy cop-out, consider—just for a moment—how trans-formative this could be in your personal relationships, in your workplace, in your neighbourhood and the other communities you belong to . . . to say nothing of a potential transformation of our parliaments.

●

Perhaps we've been looking in the wrong place for moral guidance. Perhaps the days of traditional, institutional authority are numbered. Certainly, people speak as though they are expecting less than ever from their political leaders, declining church attendance tells its own story and people were appalled but not surprised by the revelations of the 2018 banking royal commission. It's possible that some of these institutions will reform their practices to the point where they win back our trust. It's also possible that alternatives (splinter political parties, house churches, smaller financial co-operatives such as credit unions) will take over many of the roles of the traditional institutions.

Meanwhile, where might we look for inspiration?

One promising place could be the work of our creative artists—poets, writers, painters, composers. At their best, these are the people telling us our own story and reinforcing that all-important sense of interconnectedness, and even inter-dependence, which encourages us to accept respon-sibility for each other's wellbeing. Sometimes, they even seem to be sending us messages from our future, mocking the petty vanities and flagging the moral lapses that hold us back from true social progress.

But we must also look inside ourselves. The so-called 'crisis of leadership'—whether in politics, banking, religion or elsewhere—might be part of an important culture-shift in which we begin to understand that the future is in no one's hands but ours; that we are the masters of our own destiny; that we must make our own sense of our own lives.

Above all, when it comes to morality, we must decide for ourselves.

Introduction

If you're looking for someone to tell you what's right and wrong, you've come to the wrong place: this is a book about how to decide for yourself. I'm not going to preach to you. I'm not even going to try to persuade you to take more care in making moral choices (though I'd like to encourage you to refrain from making judgments about other people's choices). I'm certainly not going to set myself up as some kind of guru who has all the answers. Far from it. If I'm trying to convince you of anything, it is that you can find within yourself the answers to questions like 'What should I do?' or 'How should I live?' or even 'What's the point of trying to do the right thing?'

Your own experience has probably already taught you all you need to find the answers to such questions, since we mainly learn by doing. But you might not yet have worked out a reliable way of coming up with the right answers when you need them, and this book suggests some habits of thought to help you do that. Of course, we're all enchantingly and irrationally human, so knowing the right thing to do in a particular situation is no guarantee that we will actually do it. Sometimes our convictions are swept aside by the thundering rush of hormones, our values are confused by the clamour of the commercial marketplace, or our consciences are pounded into submission by the heavy artillery of ambition, wealth or power.

'I know what I *should* do,' you hear people say, 'but I don't know whether I have the courage to do it.' Or, 'It might be the right thing to do, but it's not what I *want* to do.'

We can usually find plenty of reasons *not* to do the right thing, even when we know what it is: most of us have experienced that uncomfortable and embarrassing gap between what we do and what we believe we should do. One purpose of this book is to help you narrow that gap; another is to suggest some practical strategies that will make it easier to work out what's right and wrong *for you*, whenever you are confronted by a moral choice. Moral decision-making is complicated by the fact that a particular course of action can seem right today but wrong tomorrow, so we must always take into account the particular circumstances of each case. Sometimes we'll find ourselves having to make rather tentative decisions in cases where moral certainty doesn't seem to be available to us or where there appear to be several equally 'right' answers to the same question. That's why we have to *decide* what's right and wrong: there are few if any moral absolutes for us to rely on.

Almost all the decisions we make have a moral dimension, in the sense that, one way or another, they affect the wellbeing of other people. When we ignore that moral dimension, we plant the seeds of our own frustration and unhappiness: peace of mind depends, at least in part, upon knowing we did what we honestly believed was the right thing at the time, knowing we were true to ourselves and sensitive to the wellbeing of anyone likely to have been affected by our actions.

If you've picked up this book because 'doing the right thing' is your goal then we're in for a rather exciting journey together—a journey that will take us from the wisdom of the ages to the cutting edge of biotechnology. Along the way, we'll examine the strange idea that people sometimes *want* to be lied to; we'll pick our way through the moral minefield of relationship break-ups; we'll find out why some people behave with less integrity in their business dealings than in their personal relationships; we'll explore the difference between 'legal' and 'ethical'; and we'll consider why it's not a good idea to confuse morality with religion.

Above all, we'll come to understand that morality isn't a set of rules or even a road map: it's a way of travelling, a mindset, a resource for the journey. 'Goodness' is not a destination; it is more like the calibration of true north on a compass, maintaining our sense of direction while leaving us free to explore whatever lies ahead.

PART ONE

TAKING CONTROL
OF YOUR LIFE

1

Freedom to choose

In everything from consumer goods to ways of living, modern Western societies offer their citizens an extraordinary array of choice. Today, within reason, you can eat what you like, live where you wish, holiday when and where you choose, marry whoever you like and divorce them at will, not marry at all, live alone or with someone else, have children or not as you please, and enter and leave sexual relationships with unprecedented freedom. It seems likely that, in the near future, you'll even be able to decide the extent to which you might prolong your own life.

Along the way, you can choose between a hundred variants of shampoo and, depending on your financial circumstances, you will probably face more than a dozen possibilities when you decide to buy your next car: even when you choose a make and model, there'll be more decisions involving colour, trim, extras, accessories and length of warranty. It almost seems as if the modern ideal is to maximise the choices available to us—as if 'freedom to choose' is all we mean by freedom, so the more choices we have, the more free we must be.

Parents often remark that their children have far more freedom than they had at the same age, and this is usually a comment on the range of choices available to their children that were not available to them: choices about courses of study, fashion, social activities, entertainment, sport, ways of communicating with each other, sexual behaviour, work . . . everything.

Perhaps inevitably, this has produced a rising generation of young people so conditioned by the range of options available to them, so bedazzled by the idea of choice, that 'flexibility' has become their watchword, 'keep your options open' their generational ethic. Their favourite question: 'What else is there?' Having grown up in a period of rapid social, economic, cultural and technological change, they have learned to postpone commitment—whether to a course of study, a job, a sexual partner, a set of religious beliefs, a political philosophy, a musical genre or a commercial brand. *Wait and see, wait and see.*

Free to choose, reluctant to judge

Such a commitment to non-commitment—such ready adaptation to change, difference and diversity—has led them to accept that virtually anything can be 'cool'. This new meaning of cool is no longer merely a label for someone who looks attractive and confident (though there is still, it's true, a magic formula, known only to the young, that qualifies people of a certain unselfconscious style to have that highly desirable label bestowed on them). 'That's cool' has come to mean not only that it's wonderful or desirable or enviably suave, but also that it's okay, it's permissible, it's acceptable . . . and it's increasingly difficult to find something that *isn't*. The new freedom to choose has produced a new reluctance to judge.

This is part of a general culture-shift away from prescription and conformity towards the idea that we are all free to choose how we shall live, and that, in a diverse and pluralistic society, judgments upon each other's choices are uncalled-for. This is a highly desirable state of affairs from almost every point of view: most religious and moral systems carry warnings against the dangerous and destructive (including self-destructive) effects of being judgmental in our attitudes towards others.

Another kind of freedom: Knowing you're right

There's another way of thinking about freedom that transcends our freedom to choose. In *The Needs of Strangers*, Michael Ignatieff discusses St Augustine's distinction between the freedom to make choices and the deeper sense of mental and emotional liberation—the peace of mind—that comes from knowing we have made the *right* choice. He examines the idea that if we 'give everyone enough income and sufficient rights, they will be free to act in accordance with their choices'. But then, echoing Augustine, Ignatieff questions whether freedom is 'a tainted good unless it is accompanied by a sense of certainty'.

Perhaps 'freedom to choose' is only half the story; the other half is feeling confident in the choices we have made, believing we are right, knowing we have chosen wisely. *True* freedom depends upon the combination of these two factors, which is why the mere freedom to choose does not liberate us from our restlessness and anxiety. We need to know that we have made the *right* choices: if we lack that assurance, we will be forever searching for more choices to make—via yet more 'retail therapy', more holidays to ever more exotic destinations, or more romances with new partners.

> *Now I've got all this choice, why don't I feel better? Sometimes when I go shopping, I feel as if there are too many decisions, too much choice. Maybe it's the same with my life—I've been married twice, but I still feel as if life should hold more for me than this.*

That's not an uncommon feeling, and it arises directly from the lack of Augustine's 'second freedom'. Perhaps the biggest challenge we face in the new era of freedom-to-choose is finding a way of *knowing* our choices are valid, authentic and wise. In our materialistic lives as consumers, it may not matter too much: most of us don't look to a bowl of cereal or a diamond ring or a new car for the deepest satisfaction life has to offer. But when it comes to moral choices, the lack of certainty that we are doing the right thing—or, at least, the right thing *for us* in the circumstances—can sap our confidence and make a mockery of the freedom we thought we had. 'Anything goes' might not be the best definition of freedom, after all, especially when you realise that we are social beings whose common humanity implies some moral responsibility for each other's wellbeing.

Is 'common sense' enough?

Most of us can recall making poor moral choices that have had an adverse effect on our life or someone else's life—sometimes for a little while, sometimes for years. The phrase 'living with your conscience' is an irritating reminder that decisions based on ethical considerations always have consequences. Once we make a moral choice, we bind ourselves to its implications, which is why the habit of thinking through the likely consequences of any action *before* we act is an important ingredient of a 'good' life.

Most of the time, we make our moral judgments on the run, relying on a kind of operational conscience we acquire and refine as a result of living with the consequences of all our previous actions. We sometimes experience this as 'intuition' or a 'gut reaction'. Many people come to the same conclusions about what's right and wrong, just as many people raised in the same culture find themselves agreeing about what is beautiful or ugly.

There are times, however, when the intuitive, operational conscience doesn't seem to be working—perhaps because we feel ourselves irresistibly drawn to do something of which we would normally disapprove, or because we feel confused and uncertain about what really would be the right thing to do in some particular situation. In such cases, we may need to reflect on the issues involved more deeply than usual, perhaps trying to identify some basic principles that may guide us to the best decision.

Is extra-marital sex ever a good idea, for instance? Should a woman be free to terminate an unwanted pregnancy? Should euthanasia be legalised? Should scientists working with biotechnology be allowed to 'play God', or is there some special meaning of 'human' that makes things like human cloning wrong? How should we weigh the need for tolerance against the need to speak up when we feel as if our personal values are being threatened by the 'alien' influence on our culture of a particular minority group? Is hypocrisy a threat to our integrity or a necessary social skill in a civilised society?

Is religion losing its moral authority?

Through much of human history, such questions were answered for us by religious institutions that linked the idea of morality to a particular set of religious beliefs: 'If you believe this, then you should do that.' Men and women of faith were assumed to be 'good' people because they followed the moral code prescribed by their particular religion—though history also records the myriad ways in which religious people have behaved very badly, often when acting in the name of religion itself. For many people, the link between religion and morality was strengthened by the promise of rewards or punishments in an afterlife, according to whether the believers in a particular religion either obeyed or disobeyed its moral code.

Religion is not dead, of course, nor will it ever be, because its comforts and consolations will always be precious to believers. It will also survive because it appeals to basic human curiosity about the numinous and eternal, and because so many people have a deep urge to believe in something or someone (ranging from a personalised deity to a mystical view of 'the universe') that transcends the pleasure, the pain and the sheer tedium of daily life. And, for some people, it will survive precisely because it absolves them of the responsibility of having to decide for themselves what's right and what's wrong in any situation that might arise. But organised religion has lost its moral authority in many parts of the world—especially in Western societies long regarded as nominally Christian—as more and more people drift away from institutional religion and seek a non-religious basis for their personal morality. The link between faith and morality, long accepted as part of the essence of religious life, has been challenged, especially in areas like contraception, euthanasia and sexual behaviour.

This may be good news. Instead of being the special province of paternalistic religious leaders, the power to make enlightened moral choices now passes to each individual, each family and each community. Liberated from the yoke of religious prescription, morality can be seen as a secular pursuit: we are not going to be 'good' because our religious beliefs demand it of us, or because our faith points to rewards in heaven, but because we want to work out a way of living that allows us to be at peace with ourselves and each other.

This is not to deny that many religious people regard their faith as a wellspring for virtuous behaviour. St James wrote that 'faith without works is dead', and plenty of Christians, and believers in other faiths such as Islam, agree with him: they regard adherence to their moral code as a direct expression of their faith. In the post-religious era, however, many non-believers are equally keen to assert that 'works without faith' are certainly not dead: their morality, *not* being based on a set of religious beliefs, is as authentic for them as any inspired by religion—perhaps even more valid, more relevant, for having been fashioned out of contemporary, personal experience rather than passed on through religious traditions born out of ancient experience.

•

The book you now hold in your hands will not unlock the meaning of life. (It's your job to invest your life with its own meaning.) It will not try to prescribe how you should live your life. Its only purpose is to help you achieve greater clarity in your quest for an understanding of what's right and what's wrong for you, in your own particular circumstances.

2

Can there be more than one right answer?

Virtually everyone believes it is wrong to kill, yet people do kill each other—in wars, in premeditated murders, in crazed massacres, in intensely personal but apparently uncontrollable crimes of passion, and in the quiet and considered circumstances of euthanasia, where people are sometimes prepared to kill those they love most deeply as a way of relieving their suffering. Mostly, they continue to think killing is wrong, even after doing it. In war, for example, we justify killing the enemy because we believe the enemy is equally intent on killing us: pausing to think that this soldier I'm about to kill is someone's son or father or husband or lover may mean that he—untroubled by such thoughts—will kill me first. By justifying the killing of other people in war, have we succeeded in making killing 'right', at least in that situation?

There are many morally ambiguous situations in which we kill each other: active euthanasia (bringing someone's life to an end by medical intervention, in order to relieve them of any more suffering), passive euthanasia (the withholding of medical treatment to people—even babies—who seem unable to enjoy even a minimal quality of life), self-defence and capital punishment. There are crimes of passion where murder seems justified—at least to some people. We'll explore such situations later but, for now, they stand as examples of the fact that, although we might assert that 'killing people is wrong', we still do it and, in particular circumstances, some of us even argue that it is right to do it.

Virtually everyone believes it is wrong to steal other people's property, but most of us do it, one way or another. We steal time from the boss by making personal phone calls at work, or by leisurely browsing on the internet when we're supposed to be doing something else. We often yield to the temptation to take something that doesn't belong to us—a pen, a book, an umbrella—because it's there, we want it, and perhaps we think our theft will be undetectable. (Many things that might otherwise seem wrong don't seem quite so wrong if we believe we'll never be found out.) Perhaps at that moment we need the object too urgently to be fussed about the proprieties, or perhaps we say to ourselves 'I'm only borrowing this' without much conviction about the need to return it.

Those who take excessive profits in the marketing of a product or service, or in the making of a business deal, are exploiting others' vulnerability to an extent that amounts to theft, especially where those being exploited are given insufficient information on which to base the decisions they are making.

Most of us would say lying is wrong and deception is bad, yet almost all of us tell lies from time to time, for various plausible reasons, and some people even manage to make a living out of deception. A car dealer might successfully conceal information about the true condition of second-hand cars; an advertiser might make exaggerated claims about the benefits of using their product; politicians might deliberately deceive the electorate—about some ministerial impropriety, for instance, or about the true state of the economy, or about secret defence arrangements with other countries—so the voters will continue to support them.

Even when we suspect someone is lying to us, we aren't always outraged, perhaps because we expect it of certain people, or certain classes of people, or because we think 'it's all part of the game'—whether the game is politics, business or sport.

Another example: monogamy is highly praised as a virtue in our society, yet many people have sexual relations with people other than their committed partners. This doesn't necessarily mean they believe the ideal of fidelity should be abandoned; it doesn't even mean they approve of their own actions, or that they've changed their minds about the desirability of people being faithful to their partners. What it means is that there are circumstances in which people of apparently unimpeachable integrity find themselves falling in love with someone other than their partner and feel compelled to act on those emotions. Though they may not say 'I'm doing the *right* thing,' they clearly believe that what they are doing is not bad enough to make them stop doing it: wrong, perhaps, but not *very* wrong; wrong in the context of a relationship that's giving satisfaction to both parties, but not quite so wrong in the context of a miserable one.

Sometimes, it doesn't mean any of that: some episodes of infidelity merely demonstrate that sexual lust (just like the lust for power or money or possessions) is such a powerful urge, it can overwhelm other aspects of our nature that normally impel us towards fidelity. In such circumstances, we may find ourselves doing things we would normally criticise or even ridicule in others; we may feel ashamed of our actions; we may live for years with feelings of guilt and remorse. *And*, being humans with a tendency to moral frailty, we may repeat, in the future, the very actions that caused such guilt and shame in the past. (Slow learners, too.)

Moral certainty is no certainty: We often have to choose

When it comes to morality, we often say one thing and do another. What this suggests is that all the principles, laws and commandments in the world won't stop us from occasionally acting in ways that seem contrary to the common good—or even to our own good. 'He was clearly on a path of self-destruction.' 'She seemed compelled to do what she did, even though anyone could have told her she wasn't doing the right thing.'

Even when we deliberately, calculatedly try to act out of self-interest—to 'please ourselves'—it doesn't always work out the way we intend.

While many partners decide, quite rationally, that leaving a relationship is morally right for them, others decide, in apparently identical circumstances, that leaving would be wrong for them. Some will decide, out of loyalty and love, to stick to a partner who has become physically or emotionally difficult to handle but who needs support and comfort; others will decide that 'life's too short' and seek a different kind of fulfilment in a new relationship—or in the apparent freedom of having no intimate relationship at all.

Some people will think staying in a demanding relationship is a dutiful, virtuous thing to do (and, in the process, they may *need* to feel that virtue is indeed its own reward); others will feel that true virtue lies in asserting yourself and your own needs, and sacrificing the needs of others to your own quest for fulfilment. Everyone has their own definition of courage: 'She had the courage to stay,' someone may remark; 'She didn't have the courage to leave him,' someone else may say of the very same person.

We sometimes feel perfectly clear and confident about right and wrong courses of action, and are then perplexed to find other people reaching the opposite conclusion in similar circumstances. It's even more perplexing when they seem as clear and confident about their position as we are about ours.

After careful consideration, some women will decide to have an unborn foetus aborted, and feel calm and confident about the rightness of their decision. Other women—or even the same women at other times of their lives—may feel that an abortion would be wrong for them. In both cases, the women might say that concern for the ultimate welfare of the unborn child was the uppermost consideration, or that their own physical and emotional wellbeing was the primary motivation.

Are you a utilitarian? (Most of us are.)

Does that mean there are several 'right' answers to the same question, depending on the circumstances? Of course it does. Whether we like to admit it or not, that's how we live: we embrace a principle and then, situation by situation, we test it against the factors operating at the time—including the strength of our own feelings—and decide whether to adhere to the principle, bend it or abandon it. For most people, the fundamental guiding principle will be something like this: we should try to promote wellbeing (or 'happiness') and prevent suffering. This is known as 'utilitarianism', and it has a long and distinguished tradition in moral philosophy, beginning with the English philosopher Jeremy Bentham (1748–1832). If we embraced this principle, we might conclude that any action intended to produce happiness or prevent suffering is 'right', and any action that produces suffering or prevents happiness—or produces more pain than pleasure—is 'wrong'.

The utilitarian principle is sometimes expressed as a desire to contribute to the common good, to maximise happiness (or perhaps 'contentment') and minimise pain and suffering, or to act in a way that has the best possible consequences *for all concerned.*

This idea of contributing to the common good or acting in the best interests of all concerned is the starting point, at least, for most ethical theories. Many philosophers would go further and say that, to be valid, any moral principle should be intended as a *universal* principle—that is, a principle we believe would be good for everyone to adopt. The German philosopher Immanuel Kant (1724–1804) expressed this by saying that we should only make moral decisions we could conceivably encourage everyone else to make in the same circumstances.

Of course, utilitarianism, like every kind of moral philosophy, is fraught with difficulty as a guiding principle because it calls on us to try to work out what *will* maximise goodness and minimise harm—in a total sense, not just for ourselves. It obliges us to calculate, to weigh up, all the consequences of an action for all the parties involved, and this will sometimes seem like a huge challenge. But the fact that it's difficult does not make it a bad principle to adopt, and it's one of the twin principles that underpin this book. (The other is that virtue, or goodness, is an intrinsically worthwhile ideal.)

Another difficulty with utilitarianism—and with the idea of pursuing virtue—is that even among people who agree that such principles should guide their moral decision-making, there are still many occasions when they will disagree about the 'right' course of action in a particular case. So the principles are never quite so neat that they can supply us all with the same answers to every moral dilemma.

Does this mean that, in practice, there are no universally valid principles at all, and that morality is an entirely subjective matter, influenced by shifting values and changing circumstances?

That question might sound as if we are on the threshold of moral anarchy. What if we were to accept the idea that there are no hard-and-fast rules about what is right and wrong? Would that mean that anything goes? Is that where postmodernism has brought us: please yourself; make it up as you go along; be sceptical of anyone talking about 'truth' or 'virtue' because they are only pushing some personal or political agenda of their own?

Yes, moral decision-making is a situational and subjective process, but this certainly does *not* mean that 'anything goes'. Moral relativism, properly exercised, does not provide an easy way out—quite the opposite, in fact. Although there might be no absolute rules to guide our every decision, no universal 'right answers', there is always a right answer for me, here and now, and it is my personal responsibility to work out what it is.

Finding that right answer will partly depend on the circumstances I find myself in, partly on the strength of my feelings about the matter, partly on the influence of other people involved, but also on the *values* I espouse—the moral attitudes and beliefs that make me the kind of person I am and provide a framework for my thinking about what's right and wrong.

3

Where do our values spring from?

Each of us has a set of values—an ethical framework—that guides our moral choices. Some values are conscious and explicit; others are rarely thought about or articulated, but just seem to be there: 'You know when something is right or wrong.' Religious fundamentalists, the 'politically correct', the pedantic, the sanctimonious and the self-righteous might want us to believe that their particular sets of values represent a superior form of morality, but any group of children in a school playground can devise a workable code of acceptable behaviour . . . and there's even 'honour among thieves'.

Values are the ideals we aspire to, the beliefs to which we attach particular significance, the essence of our desire. They are like signposts pointing to the meaning we give our lives.

Some people report that their values are embedded in the abdominal region—'The knot in my stomach is a sure sign that I'm doing the wrong thing'—while others, mistrusting their own values, need a veritable rule book to guide them. It might be the Ten Commandments (with or without the hundreds of accompanying Jewish laws prescribed in the first five books of the Old Testament); it might be a code of professional behaviour (these days, almost every company and occupational group has one of those); it might be a set of maxims handed down by parents, ranging from 'Always wear clean underwear in case you're involved in an accident' to 'If you can't say something nice about someone, don't say anything at all'.

In countries like Australia, where Christianity has been the dominant religious influence on our culture, the so-called 'golden rule' is generally regarded as the core of our moral code: 'Do unto others as you would have others do unto you' . . . or, more colloquially, 'treat other people the way you would like them to treat you'. These are fine words and noble sentiments—and they lie at the heart of most ethical traditions, many pre-dating Christianity. Society would undoubtedly be transformed if they were widely practised. But how widely are they practised, and, indeed, how widely are they even aspired to?

The primitive appeal of revenge still has many people in its seductive embrace, yet revenge represents the most comprehensive contradiction of the golden rule it is possible to imagine: if you've wronged someone, wouldn't you rather be forgiven than have revenge exacted upon you? And there's another problem with the golden rule: most people are pragmatists at heart, and they privately reinterpret the rule to mean either 'treat other people the way you *expect* them to treat you' (which might be very different from the way you would like to be treated), or, in a complete reversal of the concept, 'treat other people the same way they treat you'.

Such a tit-for-tat approach, based on the anticipation of other people's behaviour and assumptions about their motives, is bound to degenerate into a kind of dog-eat-dog, look-out-for-Number-One arrangement. The strong soon manage to convince themselves that it's okay to exploit the weak (though they wouldn't use those words) and the whole idea of morality being grounded in sensitivity and compassion collapses (though we keep mouthing the platitudes, of course).

When it comes to the crunch, most humans don't seem particularly willing or able to follow such glowingly positive precepts as the golden rule. Perhaps that's why so many of our attempts to codify morality concentrate on the negative. Rules are mostly about what we should avoid doing—'Thou shalt not'—as if the purpose of morality is to help us avoid being bad, rather than encouraging us to be good.

The more general these rules try to be, the less they seem to connect with the practicalities and specificities of everyday life. It's one thing to be told that 'lying is wrong', but what about the lie that prevents unnecessary pain, or the 'truth' that conceals more than it reveals? When we're commanded not to covet our neighbour's possessions, how does this relate to the natural human urge to do just that? (And, by the way, isn't there such a thing as harmless coveting, just as there's such a thing as harmless fantasy? Or does every form of envy—even a lurking wish to keep up with the Joneses' new Toyota—corrode the soul? What about those who envy other people's religious faith?)

In practice, few people live their lives by a set of inflexible, immutable rules. Most of us would own up to a number of general moral principles that guide our approach to 'doing the right thing' or 'living the good life'. But the idea of morality being a *relative* thing has been widely accepted as an inherent feature of any liberal, secular society. We acknowledge that the rules change from time to time or need to be applied flexibly, according to particular circumstances.

Yet there's an undercurrent of uneasiness, a kind of queasiness, that goes with all this flexibility and relativity. When people reflect on the quality of their lives—on their level of comfort or fulfilment—or on their quest for peace of mind, they often speak of a grumbling, low-level malaise, an unfocused feeling of anxiety, a sense that, in spite of economic prosperity and material comfort, all is not well. Sometimes they are merely reflecting the inherently uncertain state of the world but they are often speaking about something as specific and personal as a crisis in their sense of their own values. A recurring complaint is that there is a large and embarrassing gap between the values we *claim* to believe in and the way we actually lead our lives.

The values gap

If you ask me to tell you how I think I should live—what values I should live by—I can tell you. But don't look at my life for the evidence.

Comments like that suggest that, although people might reject the idea of hard-and-fast moral rules, they generally have some intuitive sense of how their own lives should be lived, as if they have a built-in concept of the ideal life *for them*. When they sense that their lives are falling short of their own standards—when there's too wide a gap between the ideal and the reality—they begin to feel uncomfortable. People express that idea in different ways:

I want to simplify my life, but it keeps getting more complicated. I hear myself telling people that I'm trying to cut down on the number of things I'm involved in, but when they see the way I live, I'm sure they don't believe I'm serious. I love the idea of 'simple pleasures' but I don't seem to create the opportunities to enjoy them—having friends around for a simple meal, for instance, or taking the kids for a walk along the beach in winter, without having to buy a T-shirt or video to prove we did it.

I want to slow down, but I keep running faster. I sometimes find myself feeling so stressed, I think I might blow up. I know this is no way to live, but I don't seem to be able to work out what to do about it—there are so many demands on my time, I feel as if I have no control over my own life. I'm sure my mother's life wasn't like this: she had a husband and children to look after, but she didn't have a full-time job as well, and she didn't spend her weekends driving us kids from one thing to the next. I think desperate measures might be called for—I've even considered checking myself into a nursing home for a break.

I know I should spend more time with the people I love— the people who are really important to me—but I seem to spend less time than ever with them, and half the time our contacts are limited to a phone call, or a rushed cup of coffee. Sometimes my wife and I are reduced to leaving each other notes, because we see so little of each other. I'd hate to think I was one of those fathers who never really knew what his kids were up to . . . but the other day I discovered our youngest had been away overnight on a school excursion, and I didn't even know he'd gone until he came back. I read somewhere that spouses spend an average of twelve minutes a day talking to each other, and I have a horrible feeling we've fallen below the national average. The thing is, my family and friends are my most important priority, but you wouldn't think so if you looked at how I actually spend my time. You'd think work was the most important thing in my life, followed by golf. I know it's crazy, but I don't seem to be able to do anything about it.

I don't want to be so materialistic, and I certainly don't want to raise my children to be so materialistic, yet I keep buying more stuff—and I give in too easily when the kids say they want the latest thing, whatever it is. I know I'm setting a poor example, but I keep doing it. Why is that?

Childhood should be a time of freedom and innocence, but my own children's lives are too structured and scheduled, and I realise that, half the time, it's because they have to fit in with the demands of my own busy schedule. So I'm actually creating the kind of childhood for them that I don't really believe is in their best interests—yet I keep doing it.

The question is: are these complaints serious and legitimate, or are they merely signs of superficial, transient guilt that we experience as part of the process of adapting to a busier, more complex and inherently stressful way of life? Will the values gap ultimately disappear—not because we've brought our behaviour into line with our values, but because we will have gradually, almost imperceptibly, modified our values to fit the way we live? (That's already happening to the many people who have decided that busyness is the great modern virtue: 'How are you going . . . *busy*?' they ask each other, as though a slackened pace might be a sign of weakness or failure.) Or do people feel the stretch of the values gap so keenly that they are actually going to develop strategies to change the way they live?

There'll be some of both, no doubt, but research conducted by Newspoll for the Australia Institute suggests that about 40 per cent of Australians have made significant changes to their lives in the past ten years, with the specific goal of simplifying, slowing down or 'downshifting'.

The values gap is actually a symptom of a deeper malaise afflicting modern, urban societies. That malaise can be glimpsed through two recurring themes in my own research over the past ten years.

First, many people are complaining about having lost the sense of community they once enjoyed:

The neighbourhood doesn't work as well as it used to; we don't feel as safe in our street or our suburb as we once did: we can't let the children run free the way we did as kids; we don't even know our neighbours.

For many people, the loss of a sense of community is felt even more keenly in the workplace than in the neighbourhood:

I don't enjoy work as much as I used to when you felt you were more valued as a person and when you were all part of the same big family. Loyalty is a thing of the past. The personal touch has gone. It's all about the bottom line these days, not about people.

Second, many people claim to be experiencing a dulling of their moral clarity—partly because of a sense of greater moral ambiguity and partly because of declining confidence in the idea of 'shared values':

> *People aren't so clear about what's right and wrong any more; it's harder to know what to tell your children—there seem to be more issues for them to face. There isn't the same sense of shared values we once had.*

This feeling that shared values have become harder to identify is associated, in many people's minds, with the increasing complexity of a pluralistic, multicultural society. It is not uncommon for people from an Anglo-Celtic heritage to assert that the values of immigrants from some other cultures are so different from those of the host community that there is an inevitable fragmentation—or, at least, a complication—of the moral fabric.

Others pin the blame on the decline of religious observance and the lack of formal moral instruction of children via the fables, legends and parables of religious literature and tradition (and it's true that church attendance in Australia has declined sharply over the past thirty years: only about 15 per cent of Australians currently attend church once a month or more often). Indeed, when Australians talk about their beliefs, they sometimes refer, rather wistfully, to their belief in the value of belief—as if they've lost something they rather wish they could have retained (though, as we shall see in the next chapter, this wistfulness about religious belief may be based on a perception of the church as a moral guardian rather than a source of spiritual succour).

A fragmentation of values is also seen by some people as the inevitable result of a better-educated population leading to a more open, questioning society in which young people are being taught to challenge authority and be more sceptical in their attitudes to everything.

Morality is a by-product of community

These two concerns—a declining sense of community and a declining sense of moral clarity—are not really two at all, but one: they are bound to each other by the inexorable dynamic of cause and effect.

If there is indeed a loss of the sense of community, then this would explain the loss not only of shared values but of moral clarity in individuals as well, since the moral sense is a social sense: personal relationships are the lifeblood of morality.

Our moral values spring directly from the experience of learning how to live with other people—a process that begins in infancy when we gradually and painfully learn that we are not located at the centre of the universe, that our needs are not always going to be met unquestioningly, that even our mothers have other things to do, that other people's needs have to be taken into account and their needs will often compete with ours. Family life is a source of powerful moral instruction—mostly by example rather than precept—and so are the school playground, the neighbourhood, the workplace and the wider community. Morality is a product of communal life and a well-developed moral sense in an individual is a sure sign that the process of socialisation is working.

To put it bluntly, we tend to behave more sensitively towards someone we meet if we know we are likely to see them again. Morality depends upon this idea of contact, connection and community. In traffic, for instance, some drivers, lacking a sense of 'the fellowship of the road', shout all kinds of abuse at their fellow road-users, but their tone changes dramatically if they suddenly recognise the person they're abusing: we tend to be less careful with strangers than with friends, neighbours or work colleagues.

Customers' judgments about the ethics of a business organisation are usually based on their personal experience of the organisation. How do members of the staff treat me? How do members of the staff treat each other? How does morale seem to be? How well are complaints handled? Of course, things like the reliability of the products sold and the credibility of mass media advertising will make their own contribution to the overall perception of the ethical standards of the organisation, but *personal encounters* are the acid test.

As customers, we intuitively assess the ethical tone of an organisation—a restaurant, a hospital, a supermarket, an insurance company, a car dealership—by the extent to which we feel as if our rights, needs and wellbeing are being taken seriously; the extent to which we feel properly informed about what is happening; the extent to which our transactions are transparent. It often comes down to the quality of our personal encounters with the staff: 'Am I being treated like a person with individual needs, or purely as profit fodder?' Naive though it may be, we tend to perceive personal warmth and responsiveness as symptoms of ethical integrity.

This suggests that we are unlikely to develop moral sensitivity towards other people unless we regard them as members of our community, in the broadest sense, ultimately based on our sense of shared humanity. It's easy to do this when we're talking about friends or neighbours, which is why a heightened sense of moral obligation (or, at least, moral restraint) develops more easily in a village or small town than in a poorly defined suburb in a large, impersonal city. The real test of our moral development comes when we're dealing with strangers, or with people we don't particularly like. It is our capacity to take *their* rights, needs and wellbeing into account that defines our progress towards moral enlightenment; it also defines the extent to which we can call ourselves members of a civilised society.

If there is any justification for the growing conviction that the sense of community is being eroded, then it's not surprising that so many people are reporting a growing sense of confusion about moral questions, and some uneasiness about whether our traditional 'shared values' are still intact. We don't like to feel as if we are being good on our own . . . when it comes to morality, we're in this thing together! After all, the essence of any moral code lies in the concept of *mutual obligation*. Though some heroic souls cheerfully devote themselves to the welfare of total strangers, most of us have to feel some sense of connection to other people before we're prepared to accept any moral responsibility for their well-being.

It's tempting to argue that the apparent fragmentation of society is the result of an erosion of our shared values, and it's true, of course, that changing mores help to reshape society and culture—for example, a more relaxed attitude towards divorce, or towards children being born to unmarried parents, does encourage more people to divorce, or to have children out of wedlock. But in terms of the long march of social evolution, the relationship between morality and community mainly seems to run in the opposite direction: as communities form, morality evolves. So if our moral sense is losing its clarity and focus, we should look to the life of our communities for the most likely explanation.

The fragmentation of society

Many factors contribute to the perception that communities are less cohesive than they once were.

Upheavals in our patterns of marriage and divorce have destabilised many families, fractured many social networks and disrupted the lives of many children. Approximately one-third of contemporary marriages are ending in divorce, which represents a revolution in Australians' attitudes to the institution of marriage. Here's another sign of the revolution: just forty years ago, 30 per cent of Australian women were married by the time they were twenty, and 76 per cent of all Australians—men and women—were married by the age of thirty, yet today a mere five per cent of women are married at twenty, and only about 35 per cent of men and women are married by the age of thirty. At least in the short term, such trends work against the maintenance and enrichment of traditional, local, suburban communities.

About one million dependent children live with only one of their natural parents, and about half of them migrate regularly (typically once a week or once a fortnight) from the home of the custodial parent to the home of the non-custodial parent—unplugging themselves from one parent, one household, one micro-community and plugging themselves into another, only to reverse the process twenty-four or forty-eight hours later. Again, such disruptions can be expected to have some effect on the stability of the micro-communities from which these children come and go, but they might also have some long-term effects on the children themselves. Perhaps some children who grow up with this kind of upheaval will learn to take comings and goings in their stride, adapting quickly to new situations and forging new relationships with ease. Others might react in the opposite way—feeling insecure and hesitant about forming close attachments because of a lurking fear of further emotional disruption. Some will feel lifelong gratitude to parents who continued to love and nurture them, and showed them how to be flexible and accommodating under tricky conditions; others will resent parents who seemed to place their own needs above the needs of their children. ('I feel as if my parents stole my childhood' is how some children, looking back, describe their reaction to their parents' rigid custody and access arrangements.)

It looks as if somewhere between 25 and 30 per cent of the rising generation of young Australians will never marry. Parenthood is being postponed by many couples well into their thirties, and avoided altogether by a growing number: already, 25 per cent of women are reaching the end of their childbearing years without having had any children, and this percentage is likely to increase as women in the rising generation (the 'options' generation) move through their middle years, persistently postponing pregnancy until it is too late. This increasing tendency towards childlessness, plus the decision of a growing number of women to limit their families to one or two children, has driven the birthrate to its lowest level in our recorded history: 1.7 babies per woman, and falling. More than 30 per cent of babies are now born to unmarried parents, and only about one-third of babies aged 0–4 years are cared for at home during the day by a parent. All these developments offer some challenge to our traditional ideas of family and community: they certainly imply some re-weaving of the fabric of local neighbourhoods.

When you have a high divorce rate, a falling marriage rate and a plummeting birthrate, *smaller households* are the inevitable consequence—and the shrinking household is arguably the most significant demographic fact about contemporary

Australia. It's not a sudden phenomenon: in the past one hundred years, the Australian population has increased five-fold while the number of households has increased tenfold, but that trend has been accelerating over the past thirty years. Today, more than 50 per cent of Australian households contain only one or two people and the *average* household size is down to 2.5 persons. The fastest-growing category is the single-person household, already accounting for 25 per cent of all households.

Combine that with the high female participation in the workforce (about two-thirds of mothers have some paid employment outside the home) and the consequences for the life of the neighbourhood can easily be imagined.

But this need not be bad news for communities. It's true that shrinking households contribute to the problem of loneliness, particularly among people who are living alone involuntarily through divorce, bereavement, or some other circumstance not of their choosing. Aloneness sometimes evolves into loneliness, which can lead to feelings of isolation, exclusion, alienation and despair. But many people who live alone—particularly those who choose to do so—compensate for their aloneness at home by finding ways to connect with social groups outside the home.

Upheavals in the workplace, created by the massive restructuring of the Australian economy, make a further contribution to social fragmentation, mainly through the redistribution of work and wealth that has opened up the biggest income gap we have yet seen between those at the top and bottom of the economic heap. People with full-time jobs are working longer hours, robbing themselves of valuable family and community time, while many other people either have no paid work or much less than they would like.

Financial pressure on middle- and low-income earners has fuelled the rise of the two-income household. But even among high-income earners, the two-income household is becoming the norm as well-educated women pursue their careers and as the capitalist, consumerist society works its seductive charms on us, convincing us that the endless striving to acquire more and more symbols of material prosperity is a worthwhile pursuit.

Huge salaries and other payments to senior corporate executives, out of all proportion to the salaries of other employees of the same companies, emphasise the apparently unbridgeable gap between the mega-rich and the rest of us. This, in turn, challenges our long-cherished belief in the shared values of an egalitarian society.

The inexorable march of technology always seems to proceed in the direction of community fragmentation—even in the case of the much-vaunted 'social media' that appear to bring us closer together but make it easier than ever for us to stay apart. Going back five hundred years to the invention of the printing press, we can see a classic example of how technology changes us for better *and* worse: here was a technology that transformed Western civilisation and made mass literacy possible. But mass literacy, in turn, separated author from reader and made communication a private process. The more we read to ourselves, and the more we committed our thoughts to paper, the less we talked to each other. Thus a radical (and ridiculous) idea was born—the idea that 'meaning' is *in* the words, rather than in the person using the words.

A more recent example: the motor car has brought us undreamed-of independence and mobility but isolates us in our capsules. The more we come and go by car, the more we contribute to a decline in footpath traffic in our local streets and rob ourselves of those incidental encounters with neighbours that nurture the life of the community. Many people who live in the suburbs of our major cities now say, 'We don't even know the names of the people who live next-door,' or 'We have to make an appointment to talk to our neighbours.'

The telephone encourages us to settle for conversations that rely only on the words and, to some extent, the tone of voice. Most of the richness of face-to-face encounters is lost when we communicate by phone (which, incidentally, makes it easier for us to be 'phoney' in such exchanges, concealing the things we might otherwise reveal by facial expression, posture or gesture).

Email, SMS and social media posts are perhaps the most efficient and convenient of all the systems yet devised for sending and receiving messages, yet email is so easy to use, it appears to have got out of hand: many people report being swamped by emails and daunted by the number of messages they are expected to respond to. Even Bill Gates, founder of Microsoft, has warned of the dangers of relying on email at the expense of personal contact: he has remarked that email is great preparation for a meeting, and a great way to record the outcome of a meeting, but it's no substitute for a meeting.

For some enthusiastic users of social media, email has already become something of a clunky irrelevance—too wordy, too slow and too narrow in its focus compared with the potential reach of a Facebook, Twitter or Snapchat post.

The moral hazard created by new information technology is twofold: it tempts us to confuse mere data transfer with human communication—to settle, too often, for a form of message exchange that loses most of the complexity and subtlety of face-to-face encounters—and it encourages us to rely on machines at the expense of our contacts with each other. If we come to feel more connected to online networks than to each other, this will have a negative, long-term impact on our sense of community, and on the value we place on human presence.

The first reaction: Let's regulate!

When people sense that the community isn't working as well as it should *and* that there's something of a moral decline in society, a common reaction is to look for legislative solutions: let's pass more laws, let's have more rules and regulations . . . let's *force* people to act in more morally responsible ways.

It's that kind of reaction that drives calls for more police on the beat, more CCTV security cameras, tougher sentencing of criminals, tighter censorship of media content, and more control of everything from 'our borders' to the language of racial or religious vilification. This has led to a subtle shift in our thinking about the law: we are no longer content to let the law devote itself primarily to the protection of people and their property; now we want laws to control people's behaviour in ways that are designed to encourage more morally sensitive or responsible *attitudes*. This line of thinking has produced a new kind of legislation: the so-called 'educative laws' (such as anti-vilification laws) that are designed to compel people to behave in ways that were once considered the province of personal morality.

The same motive has led many corporations and professional groups to devise formal codes of ethics, which often amount to codes of practice that tell employees or members of a profession how they should behave. Many observers of this trend have noted that such codes were not required when companies and professions operated in a more collegial way; when there was more of a sense of a business and professional community which exerted its own moral pressure on employees and members of the professions (law, accountancy, medicine, etc).

Similarly, there have been loud calls for tighter regulation of the behaviour of boards of company directors, in the wake of some spectacular corporate collapses (HIH, Ansett, One. Tel) and revelations in the 2003 and 2018 royal commissions about unconscionable behaviour by the banks and other corporations.

Such calls are understandable. When people are feeling insecure, they want security; when they are feeling uncertain, they want certainty. But tougher regulations are unlikely to bring them the comfort they want. As with any system of supervision and control, too many regulations can lead to company directors being more concerned about conforming to rules (or finding ways around them) than monitoring their own performance—particularly the ethical dimension of their decision-making.

Indeed, the *Sydney Morning Herald* has reported that tightened rules on disclosure created a 'climate of fear' in corporate Australia and were strangling information flows in the finance industry—the very opposite of the intended outcome.

Still, like the materialist's insatiable urge to possess more and more, pro-regulationists can never be satisfied: if new laws appear to be working, they use that as an excuse to call for even more of the same; if they are not, they will argue that that's because the laws are not yet tough enough.

The danger inherent in excessive regulation is obvious: more laws may make us more obedient, but they may well make us less morally responsible. When people feel they are surrounded by regulations, they begin to hunt for loopholes: the complexity of our tax laws has spawned an entire tax-advice industry dedicated to helping its clients minimise their tax by finding ways around the law. Too many laws may not turn us into lawbreakers, but they certainly encourage people to look for ways of circumventing the rules.

Some drivers, for instance, regard the proliferation of speed cameras as a challenge to find ways of 'beating the cameras'. When parents impose too many rules on their children, they are likely to arrest the moral development of their children, rather than accelerate it: the kids will look at the list of prohibited activities and say, 'If it's not on the list, it must be okay,' and that's not what we normally mean by moral sensitivity.

Morality is a quite different thing from law. In the same way as many people confuse morality and religion, we are often tempted to blur the distinction between morality and law. But the law is about dispensing justice, whereas morality is about fairness (which is not necessarily the same thing); the law is about obedience, whereas morality is about choice. That's why it makes no sense for people to defend their ethical position by saying, 'I didn't do anything wrong—I didn't break the law.' Being *legally* right is a very different thing from being *morally* right.

It's easy to understand how the confusion can arise when people are trying to compensate for their own loss of moral clarity, for their fear that 'shared values' have been eroded, and for their loss of trust in institutions that were once regarded as their moral guardians. But however well-intentioned its proponents might be, the real problem with over-regulation is that we end up giving away too many freedoms and, in the process, reduce the possibility of learning important moral lessons by making mistakes.

Sometimes we have to offend other people to learn what offends other people.

The essence of moral decision-making is freedom of choice: if that choice is limited by too much regulation, then our very sense that *moral choices must be made* will itself be diminished.

The second reaction: Let's revive 'traditional values'!

Another popular response to the fear of a moral decline is to call for a return to 'traditional values'. Let's get back to basics! Let's turn back the clock! Let's put marriage and the family back at the centre of our value system! Let's have more discipline in our schools! (Let's reinvent the Fifties while we're at it, and put women back in their place as second-class citizens!)

Sometimes, this nostalgia for traditional values is expressed in the call for a return to religion—not always by churchgoers, either. Such nostalgia is sometimes felt by those who like to know the church is there and who feel the community would be a better place if more people went to church, but who have no intention of doing so themselves.

I like to see those groups of people standing around outside church on Sunday mornings . . .

It's even occasionally expressed as a yearning for a revival of religious belief.

I wish I believed in something. I can see the value in it.
I can remember how good I used to feel when I'd been to
church as a young person.

This same kind of ache created the nostalgia for 'country life', expressed in urban and suburban Australia by the eager adoption of such rural symbols as four-wheel-drive vehicles, elastic-sided boots, chintzy sofas and 'country' everything—recipes, kitchens, bathrooms, floors, beds, bookcases and verandahs. 'We think country people have got their values straight,' city folk are fond of saying. 'That's where the real [i.e. traditional] Australia is. That's the way of life we'd love to recapture' (though without the flies, the drought, the lack of services and the vulnerability to commodity prices, presumably).

The urge to turn back the clock is perhaps most power-fully expressed in the frequency of references to 'family values', especially by politicians who are trying to tap into our anxieties and insecurities. Sometimes the term is used wistfully, as if to recall a time before the social upheavals wrought by such things as 'working mothers', high divorce, falling marriage and birthrates threw out a challenge to the stability and integrity of one particular form of family life. But sometimes it is used quite aggressively, as if to identify specific social values, which must somehow be preserved in the face of widespread family dislocation and breakdown.

So what are people thinking of when they speak of 'family values'? My research suggests they are referring to values that are not unique to family life, but that children will learn most readily in the context of a secure, accepting and responsive family environment: compassion, loyalty, unconditional love (though that is possibly unique to the parent–child relationship and is by no means always present even there), tolerance of each other's frailties, eccentricities and flaws, and acceptance of the principle of mutual obligation. This is the idea captured in the old proverb, 'Charity begins at home.'

Underlying these values is the key ingredient not only in successful family life, but in successful relationships of every kind: *the willingness to value each other for ourselves, not for the things we might do or not do.* All of us want to be valued as persons, not agents.

Putting Humpty together again

If we wish to recapture 'traditional values' or re-establish a sense of shared values, we're unlikely to achieve our goal by creating more and more rules and regulations, or by preaching about ethics. Given the close relationship between community and morality, we should probably be paying more attention to the things that make communities work—the infrastructure, the facilities, the activities.

It's no accident that at a time when people fear the moral fabric of our society is fraying, the ideal of 'village life' is being widely praised. Suddenly, everyone wants to live in a village—a retirement village, an urban village, a housing estate that, by its design and by its carefully crafted name, re-creates some of the feeling of a village. There's even a version of the traditional village being offered to people living and working in high-rise buildings: the so-called 'vertical village'. Urban planners play a crucial role in our moral development—far more influential than the role played by moral philosophers or 'morals campaigners'—by designing spaces that facilitate the incidental, unplanned contacts and interactions that nurture village life and generate the sense of belonging to a community.

In this, they will be assisted by a powerful human instinct that is being frustrated by the shrinking household. If you accept that humans are by nature herd animals—social beings—then it's clear that a household of one or two or even three people hardly qualifies as a domestic herd.

Already, it's obvious that people are looking to all kinds of other herds to compensate for the breakdown of the domestic herd: book clubs, cooking classes, bushwalking clubs, choirs, adult education classes, informal discussion groups . . . and, of course, eating out more: grazing with the herd is the simplest of all the ways of connecting (and you don't even have to 'moo' if you don't want to).

The generation of new adults known as 'Millennials' (born between the late-1970s and mid-1990s) are the most assiduous herders of all. Having grown up at a time of such rapid and turbulent social, cultural and economic change, they realise that the most precious resource they have for coping with life in an inherently unpredictable and unstable world is *each other*. Their constant use of smartphones has become a way of maintaining almost continuous contact with each other when they can't be together, but excessive use carries the risk of dulling their appetite for social contact.

Lower down the age scale, the current crop of adolescents—let's call them Post-Millennials—are showing us just how risky that dulling of the appetite for face-to-face contact can be. The US adolescent psychologist and researcher Jean M. Twenge has dubbed them the iGen, because she believes a great deal of their behaviour can be explained by the fact that the smartphone entered their lives at such an early age, their attitudes and behaviour have been profoundly influenced by their strong—and often addictive—attachment to the device.

The sub-title of Twenge's 2017 book *iGen* crystallises her research findings: *Why today's super-connected kids are growing up less rebellious, more tolerant, less happy—and completely unprepared for adulthood—and what that means for the rest of us.* She has found that adolescents' heavy use of smartphones has radically altered the way they spend their time, compared with previous generations. They are spending far more time alone in the privacy of their bedroom, sending and receiving messages on their smartphones and often, Twenge says, feeling more anxious, more socially isolated and more depressed as a result of feeling left out of what others in their circle might be doing (or, at least, claiming to be doing). Twenge notes that heavy users of the smartphone are less keen to learn to drive, less keen to start dating and less keen to become independent. 'Childhood now stretches well into high school,' she concludes.

When young people—or, indeed, older and/or socially isolated people—start to favour social media interactions over face-to-face contact, this is likely to have a negative impact on their moral formation. Making ourselves emotionally vulnerable to others through the experience of empathy (largely facilitated by eye contact) is what turns social interaction into the rich experience of human communication, and it's that kind of communication that plays a decisive role in the development of our values. When we merely transfer data between IT devices without human presence, the interaction is qualitatively different and, as Twenge's research has shown, can be socially isolating. (This is the central paradox of the IT revolution: it appears to make us more 'connected' while making it easier than ever to stay apart.) And social isolation is the enemy of moral progress.

Still, Millennials are almost tribal in their sense of connection with each other, their willingness to look out for each other's well-being, their desire to support each other and their tolerance of eccentricity and difference in each other. 'Friends are the new family' is an observation ruefully made about Millennials by many of their parents.

Their sense of identity is bound up with their herd or their tribe, rather as it is in primitive tribal cultures; their concern with privacy is far less than their parents' or grandparents'. Sharing with other members of the group is their natural tendency.

Their big message to the rest of us is clear: if you want to survive in a world that is trying to push you apart, *you need to connect*. It's a message we should attend to if we're interested in developing the ethical dimension of our lives. We need to look for ways to connect—with friends, neighbours, work colleagues and others in the various communities to which most of us belong. Yes, email is great, but companies that make heavy use of email need to create opportunities for people to meet face-to-face regularly, in order to reinforce the sense of being part of a workplace community. (Never has 'management by walking around' been more necessary than now.) Friends who stay in touch by social media need to meet, as well, whenever possible. Busy families need to set aside certain times—even if it's just one meal per week—when everyone is expected to show up, park their smartphones, and not rush off after half an hour. Neighbours who meet once a year for Christmas drinks might consider doing it a little more often.

Personal relationships create our sense of connection, and relationships are the very thing put at risk by the pressures of social and technological change. So the primary challenge is not to teach people 'values'; it is to put people back together again. The more we feel *connected* to our various communities (extended family, neighbours, friends and companions, work colleagues), the better equipped we will be to make enlightened moral decisions.

4

Compassion: Linking morality and religion

In the first and second editions of *Right & Wrong*, I attempted to draw a clear distinction between religion and morality by suggesting that religion addresses the ultimate metaphysical question 'Why are we here?', whereas morality tackles a more practical question: 'How should we live?' I also suggested that religion does its work in the interior, spiritual realm, whereas morality is a social construct. On reflection, I would not now characterise the religion/morality distinction as sharply as I had previously done. Indeed, I would now say that, for many people, religion is the wellspring of morality and that, in most societies, the religious heritage has been crucial in the formation of secular moral codes. Indeed, the ethical frameworks of most Western countries are routinely described as Judeo-Christian, as a way of acknowledging their religious origins.

In those earlier editions of the book, I conceded that many believers link their morality to their faith. But there is another, deeper reason for wanting to blur the distinction. Most religions place the idea of compassion—charity, kindness, respect, forgiveness—at the very heart of their teachings and that same idea is also at the heart of any civilised moral code. The teachings of Jesus, for example, as distilled in the Sermon on the Mount and in a series of parables, revolve around the idea of a non-judgmental, inclusive compassion that extends beyond familial and friendship circles to embrace even those we don't especially like or agree with.

The parable of the Good Samaritan (Luke 10: 30–37), is a vivid tale of prejudice, hypocrisy, social class, neighbourliness and forgiveness, told in response to a question asked of Jesus: 'Who is my neighbour?' It's the story of a Samaritan—regarded as a despised outsider by pious Jews—who cares for a Jew who had been robbed, beaten and left for dead. Before the Samaritan rescued him, his plight had been ignored by a priest and a Levite (a high-ranking religious official in the Judaism of the day). The story was therefore not only about kindness and compassion, but also about radically broadening the definition of 'neighbour'.

That is just one example of the many ways in which Christian heritage has found its way into contemporary secular ethics: the term 'good Samaritan' is now routinely used to describe a person whose charity crosses the boundaries of friendship, class or ethnicity and exemplifies unrestrained responsiveness to the needs of others.

The values of human societies tend to evolve in the direction of an ethic of compassion, since showing kindness and respect towards others—including those we don't much like or who views we disagree with—is the most rational (as well as the most self-protective) response to an understanding of what it really means to be human. Humans are, after all, social beings who need the nurture, support and protection of cohesive communities, and compassion is the fuel that drives the machinery of social cohesion.

But history shows that this is not an inevitable or universal social evolutionary process, and religion has sometimes been a positive, corrective influence, and sometimes a negative, destructive one. That potential for good *and* evil illustrates the complex nature of this thing called 'religion'. At its best, it can offer an institutional framework that nurtures our spiritual yearnings and encourages engagement with the mysteries of life, while stimulating moral reflection, reinforcing the noblest human ideals and values (through preaching, teaching and the music and rituals of faith communities), and encouraging ethical behaviour. At its worst, it can focus on its own hierarchical power structures, demand blind adherence to doctrine, stifle the personal quest for faith, and foment prejudice and closed minds.

The Australian theologian Bruce Kaye points out that the negative tendencies of institutional religion towards the accretion of power and its rigid adherence to traditional liturgical practices and doctrines can lead to confusion between what he calls 'the artefacts of religion' and the essence of

Christianity itself—a form of 'discipleship' that goes beyond moral codes to a life of noble self-sacrifice, characterised by humility and compassion. This is part of the reason why twentieth century theologians like Dietrich Bonhoeffer and Paul Tillich wrote of the desirability of a 'religionless Christianity'. Many Buddhists, similarly, would say that theirs is not a religion but a 'way of living'.

The trouble with religious dogma as a basis for morality

There are three problems with looking to religion, or religious institutions, to prescribe answers to specific moral questions, as opposed to encouraging a general disposition towards compassion.

First, religious dogma evolves more slowly than society and culture, and if you stick to outdated religious dogma, you can find yourself obeying rules that no longer make sense. Why do Jews still avoid pork, for instance? And why do some Christian fundamentalists still cling to literal interpretation of parts of the New Testament to support the idea that women shouldn't become priests, or that men are destined to be the boss in virtually every context, or that women should not speak in church, or that Christianity is the only authentic pathway to godliness? Another example: why should religious prescriptions against homosexuality, devised at a time of relative ignorance of the biological and cultural issues involved, remain valid long after these matters have become better understood? You can easily track the historical contexts for such moral prescriptions, but treating them as if they are divinely ordained represents an abdication of personal responsibility and moral sensitivity, as well as a lack of respect for cultural evolution and social progress.

It's worth remembering that religions like Christianity and Buddhism, at their purest, are based on the *rejection* of explicit moral rules in favour of self-discipline and a morally sensitive state of mind. When Jesus said, 'If you love me, keep my commandments' he wasn't referring to rules at all, and certainly not to the hundreds of commandments contained in the Old Testament; he was referring to his own 'law of love' that transcends specific moral prescriptions: 'Love your neighbour as yourself.' Presented with a clear case of a woman who had breached Jewish law, Jesus urged forgiveness rather than judgment or punishment: 'Let him who is without sin cast the first stone' (though he wasn't advocating moral anarchy: he did urge the woman to 'go and sin no more').

Second, although there are some remarkably similar moral principles enshrined in the dogma of different religions, there are also some major differences. For instance, Jews lay heavy emphasis on revenge as a morally justifiable strategy, whereas Christians advocate forgiveness rather than revenge. Buddhists and Christians praise humility as a virtue; Jews and Muslims don't. Most religious believers who attach an explicit moral code to their faith would say that their morality—like their faith—is right, and others are wrong. They would say that this is borne out not only by the strength and persistence of their religious tradition, but also by their own personal experience of living in tune with their particular 'rules'.

The attempt to equate religious faith with inflexible moral positions is complicated by the fact that people in the same religious tradition often reach different conclusions about what is right or wrong in a particular situation. The case of euthanasia is instructive: many people of strong religious faith would say they are opposed to euthanasia because of their respect for the sanctity of life and their belief that human life should never be terminated by human agency. Others *who share the same religious faith* would say they support euthanasia because of their compassion for a terminally ill person who is suffering intolerable pain or a humiliating loss of dignity.

Similar differences of opinion about war, homosexuality, divorce or biotechnology may be found among people who are apparently operating within the same religious framework. If their faith (or even their interpretation of scripture) were able to determine their position on such issues with the clarity they each claim, there would be no disagreement between them about moral questions.

None of this is to deny that religious thinkers and leaders may have a great deal to offer in helping us clarify our own thinking about moral questions. Because religion is concerned with holiness (another word for 'wholeness'), the idea of personal integrity is central to most religious practice. It is absolutely appropriate for religious institutions to offer guidance in *how* to think about moral questions; the problem lies in their trying to tell us *what* to think, as well. The *what* is precisely the thing we must decide for ourselves, if our moral lives are to have integrity. For fully-fledged moral creatures, being 'good' is never about obedience; it is about weighing up alternative courses of action and deciding which is best for all concerned, in the present circumstances.

The third problem arises when religious believers assume that their God has an active role in dispensing human justice. This leads them to blame God when things go wrong for them, or to rail against God for the injustices of the world, or—most dangerous of all—to believe that if they are 'good' in a religious sense, bad things won't happen to them. Some religious fundamentalists, for instance, believe that God 'blesses' them with good health, or marital harmony, or even material prosperity as a direct reward for their piety.

But the melancholy truth is that 'good' people are no more or less likely to suffer pain and tragedy than 'bad' people. Devout parents produce deformed babies, just as non-believers do. Deeply religious people contract cancer, are maimed in car accidents and lose their jobs. The question 'Why did God let this happen to me, when I'm a good [i.e. religious] person?' represents a failure to grasp the role of religious faith . . . though, to be fair, it's not very different from the question often asked by non-religious people: 'Why is this happening to me?'

On the available evidence, there's no such thing as a God who tries to ensure justice and fairness in the world, nor a God who distributes pain and suffering as required, merely to test the character or the patience of us mortals when we seem to be in need of 'improvement' or 'growth'. If the concept of God is to play a helpful role in our lives, it won't be by creating a moral policeman/prosecutor/judge, all rolled into one.

Believers in the more interior, personal idea of God as a loving spirit draw comfort from their faith in times of distress, solace in times of adversity, inspiration and encouragement in times of despair and depression. *Why* they suffer adversity, distress or despair is a different question altogether. Many people (including me) would argue that that's a question to which there's no answer, so it's pointless asking it—a bit like asking 'What colour is Tuesday?' The challenge is not to seek an explanation for tragedy and misfortune, but to decide how best to deal with it.

Rewards and punishments confuse the issue

People who try to use religion as a source of moral prescriptions often get caught up in the idea of rewards and punishments, both here and in a yearned-for afterlife.

It's true that some of the moral choices we make do seem to be loosely based on the idea of rewards and punishments: we'll be rewarded by peace of mind if we do the right thing; we may be racked by guilt if we don't. Weighing up such private consequences is a legitimate part of how we decide what's right and wrong. But if we introduce the idea of rewards and punishments as a *reason* for acting well, we will have not only added a dimension to the moral decision-making process that we don't need—one that might actually complicate and confuse the issue—but we will also have missed the whole point of being good and living well, which is that we ought to do the right thing because it is intrinsically right, not because we will be rewarded.

If you're operating according to a system of presumed consequences in the afterlife, this might make you behave like an angel, but it might also make you feel somewhat above the struggle, morally superior, perhaps even invincible. This is especially true if you belong to the kind of religious group that believes your faith has 'saved' you from eternal damnation, regardless of how you might behave on a day-to-day basis. The idea that God will forgive your bad behaviour may be comforting, but, paradoxically, can actually encourage bad behaviour.

Anticipation of *religiously motivated* rewards and punishments is a particularly shaky basis for moral choice. What if your faith wavers? Does that mean 'right' and 'wrong' lose their clarity for you? We shouldn't need carrots to encourage us to do the right thing, nor sticks to discourage us from doing the wrong thing. We should need neither the promise of heaven nor the threat of hell to motivate us. (In any case, most of us are perfectly capable of creating our own heaven and hell, sometimes both at once, right here on earth.)

In fact, the whole idea of rewards and punishments—temporal or eternal—is ultimately irrelevant when we are confronted by moral choices. Deciding what's right and wrong is a serious business, not to be confused by considerations of 'what I can get out of this'. If you offer your children a reward for 'being good', they may learn how to win a reward, but they may not learn what 'good' is, and they will certainly not learn about the intrinsic value in doing the right thing.

•

Perhaps it's time to re-visit the wisdom that lies behind that old, old maxim: virtue is its own reward. And if you accept that humility and compassion are the noblest of all human virtues, then any means of promoting them *as a way of life* is to be encouraged. That goal takes us beyond the institutional forms of religion and beyond the specifics of moral codes. Sometimes, the question is not 'Is this right?' but 'Is that good?'

5

So . . . why be good?

If we reject religion as a *reason* for being morally sensitive and responsible, we need some other basis for believing that a good life is better than a bad one—or, at least, why a life lived with a sense of moral clarity is better than a life that's lived in a kind of moral fog where we simply react to whatever happens to us and muddle along the best way we can.

Perhaps the only motivation we *should* need is the recognition that, as members of a community, we have a duty to each other to make the most responsible moral choices we can, so that our society can function harmoniously and we can all get on with living our lives in peace and safety. If we expect to enjoy the benefits of living in a community where all kinds of services (roads, sanitation, education, protective and medical services, public transport, mass media, recreation and leisure facilities) are only available to us because this *is* a fully functioning community, then being morally responsible is an important contribution—perhaps the *most* important contribution—we can make to social harmony and efficiency.

But that's a rational argument for doing the right thing that will only appeal to people who are already disposed to accept it. It's perfectly obvious that people who don't try to do the right thing can still benefit from living in a community. There's no test of moral sensitivity you have to pass before you are granted the right of access to public roads, schools or hospitals.

For many people, it is enough to say that we ought to do whatever we regard as the right thing, simply because we believe it *is* right. That's a powerful argument, both ethically and psychologically: once you have identified a particular action as the right thing for you to do, your sense of integrity will be eroded if you choose to fly in the face of that conviction.

One of the great strengths of that position is that it calls on us to do the right thing because of its inherent rightness (for us, at this time), not because it will bring us some reward. Of course, there will sometimes be collateral benefits—like 'feeling good about yourself'—but this is a fairly tenuous link to the idea of 'rewards', and we'd do better to leave it out of the decision-making process.

To help an old person across a busy street is a virtuous thing to do, and society benefits from having citizens who are prepared to accept that kind of responsibility whenever the need arises. But there's no automatic reward that follows: the old person concerned might be cantankerous, ungrateful and impolite, and fail to thank you for your help. It was still right to help; society was still enriched by your action.

Society might not be quite so enriched, though, if having helped the old person across the street, you then called to passers-by, 'Hey, look how I helped this old person across the street!' The desire for recognition seems to diminish the virtue of an otherwise good action. Virtue *is* its own reward, and we'd better be content with that.

In fact, when people make a fuss over the fact that you've done the right thing, you have to wonder what their expectations were: do they see you as a person who *wouldn't* normally do the right thing? When the Australian cricketer Adam Gilchrist famously 'walked' in a semi-final of the 2003 World Cup, even though the umpire had said he was not out, he was reportedly amazed by the intensity of people's reactions. Gilchrist was confident he had hit the ball with his bat and the ball had been caught, so he knew he was out. But controversy raged over whether that was the 'right' thing to do, even though it was generally acknowledged as the 'sporting' thing to do. Part of the reason for Gilchrist's astonishment at the reaction to all this was the implicit assumption that he would not normally have 'walked', especially if his team had been in a less comfortable position. (In fact, the reaction was probably based on the contrast between Gilchrist's standards and those more typical of Australia's professional cricketers, who had earned a worldwide reputation for the ugliness of their on-field behaviour.)

If we're not hoping for eternal rewards or punishments, why should we bother too much with morality, except, perhaps, as a means of securing the respect and affection of others? We might think that 'being good' helps us sleep at night, but plenty of people who cut moral corners manage to sleep soundly. So, in the end, does it matter if I am a good, honest, faithful, compassionate person or not?

Rabbi Harold S. Kushner explored that question at the end of his book, *When All You've Ever Wanted Isn't Enough*. This was his answer:

> It does not seem to make a difference to my bank account, or my chances for fame and fortune. But sooner or later . . . we learn that those are not the things that really matter. It matters if we are true to ourselves, to our innate human nature that requires things like honesty and kindness and grows flabby and distorted if we neglect them. It matters if we learn how to share our lives with others, making them and their world different, rather than try to hoard life for ourselves.

Kushner's perspective is unlikely to convince you unless you are already disposed to accept that moral imperatives have nothing to do with 'getting ahead' but everything to do with the fulfilment of the noblest aspects of your human potential. Notice that Kushner's assessment of what 'matters' is very other-directed: he sees our innate human nature as being best expressed in our willingness to share our lives with others and to contribute to their wellbeing. This coincides with the Confucian emphasis on benevolence, the

Buddhist emphasis on acceptance and compassion, and the Christian emphasis on humility and self-sacrifice. All these approaches to morality put the primary focus on the quality of our relationships with other people, and how could it be otherwise? If we understand that the moral sense is a social sense, and if we are serious about making sensitive moral choices, we will be constantly attuned to the needs of *the other*. This is why so many of us find the meaning of our lives in the quality of our personal relationships.

Taking other people seriously

The more I listen to people talking about their lives, and the more I ponder the highs and lows of human behaviour, the more I'm convinced that, in a society like ours, the most fundamental of all human needs is the need to be taken seriously. Everything else flows from that.

Other needs are important, of course. It goes without saying that our well-being depends upon being fed, clothed and sheltered; most people have a need to belong to a stable social group; and a frustrated sex drive can be famously troublesome. But if you're searching for a general explanation of people's behaviour in a modern society where such primitive gratifications are relatively easy to obtain, look no further than our deep need for recognition: all of us need some acknowledgment of our unique identity.

The mark of a civilised society is the willingness of its citizens to treat each other with kindness and respect, especially when they disagree. We enshrine this idea in our unwritten social contract, through the practice of courtesy: 'How are you?' implies much more than it asks. Good manners formalise our encounters in ways that acknowledge each other's need to be taken seriously.

The depth of this need becomes obvious when you ponder the negative, destructive stuff that flows from not having it met: rage, vandalism, cynicism, alienation, depression—to say nothing of plain unhappiness. There's rarely a simple root cause of unhappiness but, somewhere in there, you'll usually find a person who feels unappreciated or misunderstood. Even being treated (especially by a partner) as if you're someone other than the person you know yourself to be is tantamount to being ignored.

Not being taken seriously feels like the ultimate insult, and insults tend to fester and seethe, waiting for a chance to counterattack. If you've ever been shocked by the vehemence of someone's apparently unwarranted attack on you, it may turn out that, quite unwittingly, you had failed to take them seriously enough at a time when they needed your undivided attention. If you've ever seen someone behave with what looked like unprovoked anger, you were probably looking at a person whose unfulfilled need for recognition and respect finally asserted itself in a boilover that, ironically, only made things worse for them.

Why do naggers persist in their nagging, when it is such an obviously ineffective strategy? Sometimes it's because they really do believe—in spite of all evidence to the contrary—that words are like water dripping on a stone, so that if they say the same thing enough times, it will eventually penetrate the consciousness of their target audience. But naggers usually become naggers because no one has shown sufficient signs of having listened to them, perhaps even failing to pay them the courtesy of acknowledging that they've spoken. (Whether the message itself is acceptable or not is a separate question.) So they pursue their relentless quest for a response—*any* response (even irritation!)—that would reassure them that they are not being ignored.

The former ABC newsreader David Capewell wrote a heartfelt letter to his local newspaper in which he complained of not being able to find a full-time job in six years. 'What really takes the cake,' he wrote, 'is applying for jobs and getting no reply, as though I don't exist.'

As though I don't exist . . . it's a common complaint among job-seekers. Having made a huge emotional investment in an application for a job, sometimes including an interview, they are too often left to draw their own conclusions. Such uncivilised behaviour on the part of employers betrays a serious lack of understanding of our need for proper personal acknowledgment, even when the news is bad.

As though I don't exist is also the cry, even today, of women who have grown weary of feeling as if they're invisible at business meetings, or in social settings where man-to-man contact seems to exclude or devalue them. It's precisely the lack of being taken seriously as equals that first lit the fire in the bellies of the militant feminists.

If this need to be taken seriously is truly fundamental it may explain why so many people, frustrated by the lack of attention paid to them, resort to taking *themselves* too seriously. There's a certain undeniable logic in the strategy that says: 'If other people won't take me seriously enough, why not do the job myself?'

From there, it's a short step to pomposity, self-importance and the kind of navel-gazing that drives away the very people with whom they'd like to engage. This is a special hazard for people living solitary private lives: we all need someone on permanent stand-by not only to appreciate us but also to tell us when to lighten up.

Being taken seriously by someone else is like rocket fuel for the spirit, but taking yourself too seriously is like a poison. One of the best reasons for giving other people the recognition they crave (apart from their intrinsic value as human beings) is that you might discourage them from embarking on the lonely and self-destructive descent into hubris.

It's no wonder good listeners are so highly prized in our society: listening to other people—getting to know their fears, their prejudices, their values and their aspirations—is the crucial step towards understanding their needs. And it is also the thing that lies at the heart of any moral system that obliges us to accept some responsibility for each other's well-being: until we *know* the people we're dealing with, how can we be expected to take their well-being into account?

Ronald Epstein, a US medical practitioner who has written about the need for 'mindfulness' in medical practice, maintains that the key to good medical practice is to be found in full acknowledgment of the fact that the relationship between doctor and patient *is* a relationship—that is, an interaction between two complex bundles of attitudes, values, needs, prejudices, fears and aspirations. Doctors must get to know their patients as whole persons but they must also stay closely in touch with themselves as whole persons: they should take their own needs and values into account when they are trying to understand and respond to the other person's.

That sounds like good advice for all of us—not just medical practitioners. If we are to become more morally sensitive, it goes without saying that we need to be more closely in touch with each other's needs, but also with our own. Nothing distorts our moral judgment like a failure to appreciate the role being played by our *own* needs and values: hidden agendas are far more dangerous than transparent ones. This is the essence of successful personal relationships and it's the essence of morality, as well.

If 'virtue is its own reward' doesn't convince you, and you are looking for a *reason* to be 'good', try this: If we do what we believe to be right—if we are honest, courageous, compassionate, fair, faithful and just in our dealings with others—this will enrich our relationships and, in the process, give a sense of meaning and purpose to our lives.

6

The pursuit of happiness

It's easy to be sceptical about the pursuit of happiness, partly because happiness—at least as that term is commonly used in the modern world—is one of the most passive, elusive and unpredictable of emotions, but also because most people report that their most significant personal growth and development has come from pain, not pleasure. Happiness seems a somewhat vacuous focus for our all-too-brief and fragile visit to this planet and yet, when people try to define their goals, they often seek nothing more than this: 'I just want to be happy'. One of the most common remarks made by parents about their hopes for their children is: 'I just want them to be happy.'

Although it is true that some people seem almost to welcome misery and to wallow in sadness, most of us enjoy being happy and feel, when we're miserable (as we inevitably are, from time to time), that life is being unkind or unfair to us. So it's easy to see why we might think of 'being happy' as a suitable goal for our lives or even the 'natural' state to be in. But that overlooks an important truth about the experience of being human: sadness is as authentic an emotion as happiness, and the peaks of bliss and joy that visit us—fleetingly, it must be said—only make sense because they represent such a contrast with times of pain or trauma or sadness, or even with those times when we feel ourselves trapped in a tedious, dreary routine. If we're going to be realistic about the human condition, we shall have to accept visitations of sadness as willingly and as openly as we accept visitations of happiness.

In any case, ancient wisdom suggests that the selfish pursuit of happiness is actually counter-productive (rather like the fashionable quest for 'personal identity'): the more you seek it, the less likely you are to find it. That may seem a rather paradoxical statement, but it reflects an incontrovertible truth about human experience: self-centredness is rarely the pathway to fulfilment, let alone enlightenment.

The picture of someone who always gets their own way is not a picture of happiness: the restlessness that leads people to constantly seek new or better forms of gratification is likely to work against the achievement of the very contentment they seek. 'Learn to want what you have' sounds like good advice (though it shouldn't be interpreted as discouraging people who wish to rise above crippling poverty or disadvantage). 'I had the advantage of disadvantage' is a statement that makes a rough kind of sense: 'there is no education like adversity,' said Benjamin Disraeli. Echoing that sentiment, the US sociologist Robert Merton (pioneer of the now-ubiquitous 'focus group' as a market research tool) regarded his poor and disadvantaged childhood in the slums of Philadelphia as providing him with a good start in life, because, according to his obituary in the *Economist*, he had access to 'every sort of capital' except money.

Facing, accepting and dealing with our present circumstances, however limited they may be, is more likely to lead us to a sense of peace and fulfilment than constantly striving to get what we think might make our life richer, more comfortable or in some other way 'happier'.

Would it be uncool to mention 'virtue'?

The Greek philosopher Aristotle (384–322 BC) taught that the ideal life was the life of *eudaimonia*, a word usually translated as 'happiness'. But he was certainly not advocating a life devoted to the maximisation of sensory pleasures—nor would he have regarded as 'happy' a person living in a fool's paradise, so disengaged from the real world as to be deceived into believing things are better than they really are. For Aristotle, 'happiness' meant something rather more serious than the experience of pleasurable sensations: his brand of happiness involves acting in accordance with reason, living virtuously, fulfilling one's sense of purpose, being fully engaged with the world and, in particular, experiencing the richness of human love and friendship.

Marcus Aurelius (121–180) had much the same idea in mind when he wrote in his *Meditations* that 'a man's happiness is to do a man's true work'. Helen Keller (1880–1968), the deaf and blind American scholar, put it like this in *The Story of My Life*: 'Many people have a wrong idea of what constitutes true happiness. It is not attained through self-gratification but through fidelity to a worthy purpose.' Immanuel Kant argued that 'morality is not properly the doctrine of how we make ourselves happy, but how we make ourselves worthy of happiness'.

The prospect of living in harmony with certain virtues appeals to most people who are serious about morality and, like the varieties of utilitarianism, it permeates the thinking of professional philosophers. We may disagree about the particular characteristics of human behaviour that qualify as 'virtues', but the very fact that we believe in the *idea* of virtue may help us when we're trying to decide for ourselves what's right and wrong. It's not just a simple case of striving to maximise happiness and avoid pain for all concerned; it's also a matter of trying to behave virtuously—to *live well*.

Buried deep in our folklore is the idea of the so-called 'cardinal virtues'. In scholastic philosophy, the original list contained four virtues: justice, prudence, temperance and fortitude. Under the influence of Christianity, three others were added—faith, hope and charity—making up the classic seven cardinal virtues to offset the traditional seven cardinal or 'deadly' sins: pride, envy, sloth, gluttony, greed, wrath and lust.

Although the original four cardinal virtues have some-times been described as the 'natural' virtues, the truth is that, for most of us, virtuous behaviour doesn't come easily: we have to be taught—by wise elders, by the example of other people behaving virtuously, and by our own experience of the consequences of our actions. We have to practise if we are to become good at behaving virtuously, since practically everyone who's ever thought about it regards virtue as involving, to some extent, the postponement or denial of selfish impulses. Behaving virtuously may help us achieve some degree of *personal* contentment (and it's true that Aristotle emphasised the value of virtues to those who possessed them), but the *societal* approach to morality being taken in this book would lead us to regard the idea of living virtuously as being primarily about making some contribution to the common good.

The Scottish philosopher David Hume (1711–76) developed a list of characteristics he regarded as virtuous, placing special emphasis on those that were beneficial *to others*—things like benevolence, justice and fidelity, but also less grand qualities like politeness, modesty and decency. He also included many virtues he regarded as being mainly beneficial to those who possess them—discretion, industry, frugality, strength of mind, cheerfulness, courage—though his attempt to distinguish between 'good for us' and 'good for others' rather emphasises the blurriness of such a distinction. Being industrious or cheerful, for example, may make me feel better about myself, but it also has some obvious benefits for the community.

The contemporary French philosopher, André Comte-Sponville, offers us a more wide-ranging list of eighteen virtues in his book *A Short Treatise on the Great Virtues*: politeness, fidelity, prudence, temperance, courage, justice, generosity, compassion, mercy, gratitude, humility, simplicity, tolerance, purity, gentleness, good faith, humour and love. His treatment of humility—described by an earlier French philosopher Simone Weil (1909–43) as 'the queen of virtues'—is particularly engaging: 'Humility . . . even doubts its own virtuousness: to pride oneself on one's own humility is to lack it.' Yet, as Comte-Sponville points out, that teaches us something about the very nature of virtue: 'Virtue is nothing to be proud of . . . Humility makes the virtues discreet, unself-conscious, almost self-effacing.'

We don't have to agree about which items should appear on some precise list of virtues; we only have to accept that there is such a thing as 'virtuous behaviour' and, with even a rough-and-ready sense of what that might be, carry that idea with us into the process of trying to decide what's right and wrong *for us*.

We've already seen that followers of Confucius regard benevolence—having an essentially charitable, compassionate attitude towards other people, and a desire to seek *their* happiness—as the highest of all the virtues. Buddhists, similarly, believe that their highest goal is to develop an attitude of compassion to all, without hoping for anything in return. It doesn't take much effort of the imagination to see how the world would be a better place if we were all disposed to adopt such an attitude in our dealings with each other. But, as Buddhists and Christians emphasise, the probability that we might also feel better about ourselves should be regarded as a collateral benefit rather than the reason for behaving benevolently.

Although it may seem cavalier to suggest that we can aspire to behave virtuously without having a definitive list of what counts as virtues, most of us, in practice, have little trouble recognising virtue when we encounter it. It would be surprising if you felt in any doubt about whether kindness, honesty, courage, faithfulness or fairness should count as virtues (particularly when you contrast them with unkindness, dishonesty, cowardice, unfaithfulness or unfairness).

In our culture, virtue is actually one of the least mysterious concepts: many utilitarians, for all their apparent rationality, would have at least a sneaking regard for the idea that virtue is worth pursuing, even when it might *not* produce the greatest happiness for the greatest number. At the extreme, we may well admire a person who is prepared to sacrifice her life for a matter of principle, even though her death might not produce a perceptible increase in the general level of happiness—it might, in fact, provoke great grief and misery among those who loved her. Less dramatically, many people have terminated triangular love affairs in the name of virtue, finally deciding that their happiness in the relationship, no matter how intense or fulfilling and no matter how well hidden from those who might be hurt or offended by it, was bought at too high a moral price.

Even when we seem to be causing no pain to anyone else, rejecting or ignoring the ideal of virtuous behaviour can generate intolerable tension within us, whether in the context of a love affair, a business deal or an election campaign. Pursuing our own happiness in defiance of our virtuous impulses will, ultimately, either undermine our wellbeing through the growth of a deeper unhappiness, or corrode the sense of virtue within us.

Such corrosion can easily happen, by the way: you *can* become immune to your own sense of virtue. If you keep brushing aside the nagging voice of conscience for long enough, and if you mix with the wrong crowd—studiously avoiding exposure to the example of virtuous people—your psyche will gradually adapt to a new set of values that better match your non-virtuous behaviour.

You might start by believing something is wrong, then you keep doing it under the weight of social pressure, perhaps, or to secure a financial advantage, or to score a political point, and eventually you come to think it's probably all right or, at least, since so many other people are also doing it, it can't be too bad. 'Social proof'—allowing ourselves to be influenced by the example of others—is a powerful instrument of moral formation (for good or ill), which is why our choice of friends and colleagues is crucial. If you spend all your time with self-centred, materialistic hedonists, moral corner-cutters and dollar-chasers, you will soon come to feel that such attitudes are normal: from there it's a short step to believing they can be justified or even that they are right.

Imagine the case of a schoolboy who regards himself as being basically honest, but who suffers from loneliness and is having trouble being accepted by the other boys. Gradually he finds acceptance within a particular group of boys who don't happen to share his view of the morality of stealing. After school they often visit the local shops and engage in shoplifting as an act of bravado. Desperate to be accepted by his new-found friends, the boy goes along with them and, under pressure from the group, he, too, steals something from a shop. This makes him feel guilty: he is stressed by the tension between what he believes (shoplifting is stealing; stealing is wrong) and what he has just done.

As time goes by and his shoplifting becomes habitual, the boy finds that his guilt recedes and the tension between his values and his behaviour is reduced. Now he's prepared to say to himself, 'Shoplifting is not the same as stealing—no one really suffers—it's just harmless fun.'

The psychology of this is clear: our attitudes tend to grow out of our own experience. New experiences reshape our attitudes, and that isn't always a positive process. Contrary to conventional wisdom, most changes in our behaviour are brought about not by a 'change of heart' but by changes in our circumstances that push us to act in new ways—peer pressure, falling in love, divorce or bereavement, unemployment or a new job, illness, etc. Under the pressure of such changes, we may find ourselves behaving in ways that contradict the values we were once sure we believed in.

Nevertheless, consciously reinforcing our own commitment to the ideal of virtuous behaviour can sometimes act as a bulwark against such pressure. If we regularly remind ourselves that we really do regard faithfulness to a sexual partner as a virtue worthy of our respect, we are more likely to acknowledge that we would feel diminished if we were unfaithful (though hormones often prove stronger than beliefs). If, when contemplating a business deal, we remind ourselves that we really do believe in avoiding conflicts of interest and that our sense of our own integrity would be threatened if we were to water down that conviction, this will minimise the temptation to do something that would compromise our virtue (though money, like sex, can be a powerful persuader).

The point is that once we start thinking of virtue as adaptable, or disposable, it can begin to lose its moral force. Diogenes Laertius (400–325 BC), Greek biographer of ancient philosophers, had this to say about the place of virtue in our moral lives:

> One ought to seek out virtue for its own sake, without being influenced by fear or hope, or by any external influence. Moreover, in that does happiness consist.

That 'moreover' defines the point at which the *moral idealist*, devoted to the pursuit of virtue, meets the *pragmatic utilitarian*. Virtue *is* its own reward, but there's a bonus: the sense of contentment, fulfilment and peace of mind that virtuous behaviour brings.

The question is: Whose happiness?

There was once a rule at a Sydney boarding school that required girls at the dining table to restrain themselves from asking for something to be passed to them: they had to wait for it to be spontaneously offered to them by someone else. I don't know whether that rule has survived, but it had a serious point. It was a way of teaching those girls that the pathway to personal fulfilment is not straight: you achieve your goal indirectly, by first attending to the needs of others. The more assiduously you pass the salt to everyone else, the more likely it is that someone will eventually decide to pass it to you.

If that sounds a bit too calculating, so be it: this was meant to be a training ground for adolescent girls, after all. Even the so-called golden rule has always had a collateral benefit buried in the sub-text: 'do unto others as you would have them do unto you' might sound like unbridled altruism, but there's a strong implication of reciprocity in there. If you treat others the way you'd like them to treat you, you improve the chances that they will indeed treat you the same way.

But reciprocity is a moral minefield. If you treat others well only *because* you expect reciprocal treatment, that brings you dangerously close to exploitation, and the satisfaction you yearn for is likely to elude you. The trick is to embrace the central paradox of human happiness: we are generally at our happiest when we seek the happiness of others. 'Look out for Number One' was always a dark seductive con.

'I've never been happier' is the almost universal cry of people who perform voluntary work in the service of the disadvantaged: preparing meals for the poor, reading to the blind, visiting the sick and lonely, or helping to relieve suffering, hardship, poverty or despair in any way. It's also the experience of those working in professions like teaching, nursing, medicine and counselling, who choose to focus on the well-being of their pupils, patients or clients, and who regard remuneration as a peripheral issue.

The pursuit of happiness, it turns out, *is* a worthwhile exercise, provided we remember whose happiness we're pursuing. Seeking the happiness *of others* is a noble pursuit. Perhaps that's the first step in the long journey to personal, and ultimately global, peace.

Here's how the English poet, critic and lexicographer, Samuel Johnson (1709–84), put it:

Happiness is not found in self-contemplation; it is perceived only when it is reflected from another.

7

Moral mindfulness: Pathway to moral clarity

'The unexamined life is not worth living,' wrote Plato and Aristotle, over 2000 years ago, quoting Socrates. That has always sounded a bit harsh to me: surely there are millions of people in the world whose limited mental capacity or tough circumstances make the 'examination' of their lives either impossible or irrelevant. It was all very well for Ancient Greek philosophers—Socrates, Plato, Aristotle—but not everyone has the luxury of time, the intellectual equipment or, perhaps, the encouragement to examine their lives, yet who can say their lives aren't worth living?

Still, you're reading this book, so you are presumably the kind of person who is attracted to the examination of your life, which means you already possess one of the two prerequisites for achieving a state of heightened moral sensitivity: *curiosity*. The other prerequisite is *courage*. If you are serious about accepting personal responsibility for the moral choices you make, you will need a huge dose of courage, because you are going to be called on to do some things you would rather not do—and, more painfully, to refrain from doing some things you would very much like to do. You might also find yourself obliged to take stands that will not always be popular with family, friends or colleagues, but deciding *for yourself* what's right and wrong may sometimes entail unpopularity.

Of course, this doesn't mean you will be making moral decisions in a social vacuum. On the contrary, as we have already seen, we hew our moral code out of the often-painful experience of learning to live in a community. Nevertheless, there will be many occasions when we will decide, on the basis of our own experience and our own private reflections, that something is right or wrong *for us*, even though other people—including people close to us—may reach a different conclusion.

When my husband told me he had found a way to minimise our tax by setting up a family trust, I just felt it was wrong. We were going to be able to split my husband's income between us, and the kids were going to be employees—their school fees were going to be treated as salary payments to them . . . that kind of thing. I couldn't feel comfortable with it because it was a scheme to pay less tax—it wasn't something we would have thought was a good idea otherwise. Actually, I happen to believe we should all pay our fair share of tax, and I've always taught the kids that. So we had this huge row. Everyone in his family thought I was mad, but I finally convinced him. Later, there was a great political fuss about family trusts and I think the kind of thing my husband was contemplating became illegal. So I felt vindicated, I suppose. But I still would have thought it was wrong for us, even if it was legal. Other people manage to do that kind of thing and not turn a hair, but I couldn't sleep at night if I thought we were doing something questionable.

My mother couldn't understand why I didn't have an abortion when I was pregnant with Tom. I already had three children and we hadn't planned a fourth. Bob was working harder than ever and was overseas a lot, and my health wasn't great. Also, I'd had an abortion before I was married, so she assumed I didn't have any moral qualms about it. I was fine about it all those years ago but, this time, it just felt wrong for me. I couldn't do it.

My girlfriend was selling her car and she knew it had this fault that she couldn't afford to have fixed. She wasn't going to mention it to any prospective buyers and I thought that was wrong. I thought anyone buying that car had a right to know that it would eventually need to have this work done on it. But she said it was a case of 'buyer beware' and she wasn't obliged to mention it. She said everyone who buys a second-hand car knows they are buying someone else's trouble. I threatened to tell anyone who came to look at the car what was wrong with it, which I realise now was really confronting. Anyway, we split up over that—well, not just over that, I suppose, but that brought things to a head. Once I realised she was prepared to be dishonest over a thing like that, I felt I couldn't really trust her. She just thought I was unreasonable.

Though we speak easily of being 'mindful' of something—usually meaning no more than that we will bear it in mind—the term 'mindfulness' has a special meaning that comes out of the Buddhist tradition. In *Awakening the Buddha Within*, Lama Surya Das describes mindfulness like this:

> Pure mindfulness is relaxed, open, lucid, moment-to-moment present awareness. It is like a bright mirror: nonclinging, nongrasping, nonaversive, nonreactive, undistorting . . . Present awareness and mindfulness implies an understanding of what we are doing and saying.

He points to the similarity between mindfulness and many contemporary aphorisms: 'let go and live in the moment'; 'be present'; 'live a conscious life'; 'be in touch with your feelings'. In the Buddhist tradition, the art of mindfulness is acquired through meditation that, according to Surya Das 'explores, investigates, unveils, and illumines what is hidden within and around us'.

Moral mindfulness borrows something from that approach, and from the Aristotelian concept of *contemplation*. To quote Jonathan Barnes in his introduction to the 1976 Penguin edition of J.A.K. Thompson's translation of *The Ethics of Aristotle*:

> Contemplation is something like a review or survey of existing knowledge; the contemplator is engaged in the orderly inspection of truths which he already possesses . . . bringing them forward from the recesses of his mind, and arranging them fittingly in the full light of consciousness . . .

When it comes to the practice of moral decision-making—deciding what's right for you—the synthesis of meditation and contemplation involves a threefold discipline:

- being fully aware, moment by moment, of the ethical dimension of whatever you are doing;
- taking into account what you have learned from previous experience in similar situations;
- imagining what the consequences are likely to be, for all concerned.

Moral mindfulness is a habit of the mind—or, perhaps, a habit of the heart—that can be acquired by constant practice, fuelled by the desire to live a better life and to make the world a better place. To develop the art of moral mindfulness, you must *care* about the difference between right and wrong and be passionate in your determination to make sound moral decisions.

Soul work?

It might help to make sense of the idea of moral mindfulness by thinking of it, not necessarily in a religious sense, as the work of the 'soul' or 'spirit'. In *The Gutenberg Elegies*, US critic Sven Birkerts uses 'soul' to signify inwardness: 'that awareness we carry of ourselves as mysterious creatures at large in the universe. The soul is that part of us that smelts meaning and tries to derive a sense of purpose from experience.'

To which we could add: soul is that part of our being that aspires to do good, that recognises and appreciates truth and beauty, and gives us our capacity to behave with benevolence even when it would seem more natural for us to behave self-interestedly. When you meet someone, you can sometimes sense whether their soul (in Birkerts's secular sense) is being developed or neglected: the rampant materialist who is always 'looking out for Number One' and has a constant eye to 'the bottom line' is unlikely to be a person who has achieved mindfulness, or even aspires to do so. The out-and-out hedonist, bent on maximising personal pleasure, will be too busy seeking the next source of stimulation (and the next, and the next) to be responsive to the needs of other people. Such people seek constant distraction of one kind or another—almost as if to keep the possibility of mindfulness at bay. By contrast, we easily recognise the person who seems sensitive, attentive and responsive as a person with 'soul'.

This way of describing soul might sound more like poetry than psychology, but it reminds us that moral mindfulness is a special state: not just thinking reflectively (though it is that); not just carefully weighing up all the options (though it involves that); not just being alert (though that is certainly part of it, as well). When we are being mindful, we are being intensely introspective, self-critical and evaluative, yet, paradoxically, our whole orientation is towards others. We only enter into a state of moral mindfulness *because of our concern for the well-being of someone else.*

Stimulating moral mindfulness by 'tests'

Some people find it a useful discipline to use quite formal tests to guide the process of moral decision-making. For instance, members of Rotary Clubs (the international community service and student exchange organisation) use a *four-way test* of 'the things we say and do':

- Is it the truth?
- Is it fair to all concerned?
- Will it build goodwill and better friendships?
- Will it be beneficial to all concerned?

Those are good questions because they encourage us to think beyond specific moral prescriptions or rules. They point to some general principles we might apply when faced with a tricky decision, and they offer us a framework for examining the underlying moral issues.

Another favourite test—especially among business and professional people—is the *test of public exposure*: 'How would I feel if this conversation were being broadcast? How would I feel if my actions were shown on national television? Would I be proud of myself? Would I be confident of defending myself if a TV interviewer questioned me about the moral justification for what I had done?'

Some parents use a particularly tough version of the exposure test: the *tell-the-children test*. 'Would I willingly tell my children about this? How would I feel if they found out about it? Would they be proud of me? Would they be embarrassed? Would they be ashamed of me, and would I be ashamed of myself in front of them?' If you're not a parent, you might devise another version of the same test, involving your partner, your parents, close friends, colleagues at work, or someone else whose reactions would matter to you. One person I know says she always imagines her mother standing beside her when she is facing a moral dilemma.

Following the philosopher Immanuel Kant's idea that we should only do what we could encourage everyone else to do, some parents apply another test: '*Would I encourage my children to do what I'm thinking of doing*, if they were in similar circumstances in the future?' In other words, am I setting an example I would actively encourage my children to follow? (Again, you don't have to be a parent to use this test, but it's a particularly searching version of the Kantian approach.)

Then there's the *sniff test* which involves making a careful assessment of the situation—sniffing it out—and seeing if anything about it strikes you as being a bit 'on the nose'. If you detect a whiff of conflict of interest, or the stench of a dodgy deal, or the faint smell of unethical practice, think again. If something strikes you as 'fishy' when you're exploring the moral implications of a proposed course of action, it's important to acknowledge that. Moral queasiness should never be ignored.

And then there's the *death-bed test*: 'How would I feel about this action when, on my death-bed, I was reflecting on the way I had lived my life? How would I feel, for example, about a business decision that involved increasing my profit but went against my moral inclination, or a decision to terminate a relationship without being honest about my reasons for doing so?'

The point about all these tests is that they do not present us with a series of legalistic rules or commandments; they are not like 'codes of practice'; they do not involve prescriptions about how we should behave in specific situations. They are designed to encourage moral mindfulness—they call on us to *think through* the likely consequences of our actions, not only in terms of our own sense of personal integrity, but also by imagining how they would look to our children, our parents, our friends or colleagues, or the world at large.

Even tougher tests can be applied. Any person in search of moral clarity might find these four super-tests useful, as well:

- Will *anyone* be harmed by this action and, if so, can I avoid that harm?
- Would I do this if it were *the one and only action* by which other people were going to judge my integrity and write my epitaph?
- What values are implied by this action—and do I recognise them, or 'own' them, as *my* values?
- *Is there too much in this for me?* Is the benefit to me clouding my judgment about the likely effects on others?

Such super-tests will inevitably put pressure on us, but they can play a useful role in encouraging the introspective, self-critical attitude that is essential to moral mindfulness.

Hard-line utilitarians might set themselves a cooler, more rational test: does this action maximise pleasure and minimise pain? In *Practical Ethics*, the Australian philosopher Peter Singer puts it like this: 'at some level in my moral reasoning I must choose the course of action that has the best consequences, on balance, for all affected.'

The utilitarian's difficulty lies in making an accurate assessment of those 'best consequences' for all affected. For a start we need to acquire some understanding of how 'all affected' might view the consequences for them. Look how often explorers, invaders—and even religious missionaries— have blundered into foreign cultures with the objective of 'doing good', only to founder on their own ignorance of what would be beneficial for all those involved. For Australians, the Stolen Generations of Indigenous children 'rescued' from their parents to be raised by white people is a particularly harrowing example of people from one culture having a misguided, and possibly arrogant, sense of what's best for people from another culture.

Any strategy designed in a spirit of benevolence must pay sensitive attention to the needs, values and aspirations of all those likely to be affected by its outcomes. Moral mindfulness is how we try to anticipate all that.

Another way of describing moral mindfulness is to say that it is a way of stoking the moral engine we call 'conscience'. All these tests are like training sessions designed to increase our capacity for moral reasoning, to sharpen our moral reflexes and to give us a greater sense of moral clarity. Meditation, contemplation, introspection, 'sniff' tests . . . these are all well-proven strategies for putting us more closely in touch with the meanings we attach to our own lives—the values we want to live by—so that, when the crunch comes, we will seem to know the right answer, almost intuitively. As Lama Surya Das puts it in *Awakening the Buddha Within:*

When confronted with different points of view of what is right . . . remind yourself that your own conscience is the main judge of your actions. Of course we can always learn from others, but finally each of us can only trust our own intuitive heart.

What is this thing called 'conscience'?

Sigmund Freud called it the 'superego'—an aspect of our personalities that acts like the chief censor, the judge, the big brother or sister or parent who keeps an eye on us and raises a stern eyebrow when we're stepping out of line. For Freudians, the superego is derived from the Oedipus complex, named after a figure in Greek tragedy who unknowingly kills his father and subsequently marries his own mother (that's the sort of stuff that goes on in Greek tragedies). Freud argued that children typically go through an Oedipal phase where they unconsciously yearn to kill one parent—fathers for boys, mothers for girls—in order to have unrivalled access to the affections of the other. In Freudian theory, the superego is the result of this early-childhood complex being resolved: we abandon the urge to eliminate the parent who is in the way and, instead, submit to parental authority and begin incorporating parental prohibitions into the development of our personality. On this view, the process of moral formation is heavily influenced by our desire to please the parent who was previously threatened by our Oedipal impulses. The superego is therefore part unconscious parent-pleaser and part policeman, waiting to punish us (through feelings of guilt or shame) when we transgress against the moral rules we inherited from our parents.

Some people take a more mystical view of the conscience than that, seeing it as evidence of the 'divine spark' within us. Many religious believers who have rejected the notion of an 'out-there' divinity—a Creator God, for instance, a Supreme Being or an omniscient judge of mankind—still profess faith in a 'God within', a personal 'life force' that stimulates our most noble impulses, causes us to act out of pure altruism (at least sometimes) and guides our sense of right and wrong. For mystics, the act of meditation is a way of getting in touch with this 'God within', and that idea is closely connected with our secular concept of moral mindfulness.

But perhaps we need neither a Freudian nor a mystical explanation for the operation of the conscience. We certainly don't need to conceive of it as some black box of moral wisdom, plugged into us at a certain stage in our development and supplying us, on demand, with all the right answers.

Why not think of 'conscience' as another name for *moral memory*—that part of our memory-bank in which all of life's moral lessons are stored, including those taught to us explicitly by our parents and other guardians, and those learned implicitly through the more persuasive medium of personal experience. This is where we 'file' what we have learned about such things as the reactions of other people to one of our lapses into self-centredness, or the consequences of an occasion when we acted unfairly or dishonestly, or the emotional charge we got from acting in a way that reinforced our sense of personal integrity. It's all there, just like memories of a family picnic, a first kiss or a good movie. And just like a family photo album, we can sift through those memories at any time, reflect upon them, interpret them and make fresh sense of them in the light of more recent experience.

Perhaps that makes the operation of the conscience sound rather rational and mechanical, which it isn't. Some researchers believe it is more realistic to think of the brain as a gland than a computer and it is certainly the case that our moral memories, like most other memories, are strongly tinged with emotional colour. We don't merely remember the 'facts' concerning the consequences of a particular act: we may well recall, with even greater clarity, the feelings and sensations that accompanied the act and its aftermath. I may remember telling a lie, perhaps, but I will probably recall with even greater intensity how I *felt* about telling that lie, both at the time and afterwards, particularly if I felt ashamed of myself. (Shame is a highly charged emotion and its recollection can be a powerful teacher.)

Moral learning seems to take rather longer than other kinds of learning, and recent brain research suggests there may be a biological explanation for this. US adolescent psychologist JoAnn Deak points out in *Girls Will Be Girls* that the frontal lobes—where fine moral judgments are processed—mature more slowly than most other parts of the brain, which is why young people are often erratic in their moral judgments: 'Combine immature frontal lobes with hormones that affect body sensations. Hormones and social pressure say yes, and the frontal lobes are not yet strong enough to resist or wise enough to argue.' One implication of this is that young people need more guidance and support than they think they do while they are learning how to recognise and process the moral lessons their experience is teaching them.

You can learn about the causes of World War I well enough to pass an exam on the subject with the appropriate amount of study and preparation. But learning how to decide for yourself what's right and wrong—as opposed to learning what your parents approve of, or what other people think is right and wrong for them, or what someone else might want you to do—is a slow and often painful process. It is quite common for people to feel as if they are only beginning to develop moral confidence as they move into their thirties, the very time when the frontal lobes are normally beginning to reach maturity. Until then, through all the biological and emotional upheavals of adolescence and early adulthood, most of us are feeling our way and often relying on external signposts to guide us.

In any case, the getting of wisdom is a lifelong process. Mature frontal lobes may equip older people to make fine moral judgments, but this doesn't mean they will always get it right. There's no on-board computer that stores all the relevant data and spits out the right answer every time. Even with mature frontal lobes, new experiences constantly throw up new challenges to our moral certitude: we seem to know what's right, then we're not sure, then we find ourselves acting in ways that have undesirable consequences for us or for other people, and we realise the journey to moral enlightenment is never quite over. Our ideals seem always to be just beyond our grasp.

But the moral memory-bank—the conscience—is being enriched by all this experience and, as time goes by, its voice grows louder within us (unless we've deliberately developed techniques for silencing or even killing it, as people sometimes do). To remain active, the conscience needs our permission and encouragement: we have to *want* to make wise moral choices if we're going to be able to make them. But even motivation isn't enough to get us there. As with physical fitness, moral fitness demands constant practice.

Beyond tests, beyond conscience . . .

Even when we are committed to doing the right thing, and even when we desperately want to make a decision that is in the best interests of all concerned, we may still need something beyond our own moral reasoning, no matter how painstaking it may be, to illuminate the right answer for us. Tests are useful, and the 'gut reaction' of conscience can be quite reliable, but sometimes we yearn for an external beacon to guide us—some ideal standard against which we can test each decision we make. That is why so many people seek refuge in rules and regulations that promise to relieve us of the difficulty of having to choose: the more precise the rules, the less we have to take responsibility for our own decisions.

In *The Sovereignty of Good*, Iris Murdoch (1919–99), the English philosopher and novelist, offers us a better alternative: echoing the work of Plato, she urges us to *imagine* an ideal 'moral standard' as a way of inspiring and encouraging ourselves to make careful moral judgments. She refers to the hazards of giving blind obedience to an institution like the church, but she also recognises the hazards of simply looking within oneself for moral answers: 'Self is such a dazzling object,' she says, 'that if one looks *there* one may see nothing else.' So Murdoch encourages us to think of the ideal of goodness, and to strive towards it, even without a precise definition of what that ideal might be, and without an infallible moral compass to guide our every step:

> So long as the gaze is directed upon the ideal the exact formulation will be a matter of history and tactics . . . Where virtue is concerned, we often apprehend more than we clearly understand and *grow by looking*.

In other words, contemplating virtue can get you there. The idea that we 'grow by looking' is in harmony with many religious and moral traditions, and with contemporary psychological theory: even sports psychologists encourage their charges to visualise ideal performances as a way of improving their actual performance. Musicians, painters, teachers, actors, dentists, business executives . . . anyone can benefit from the discipline of *imagining* themselves achieving an ideal outcome.

To amplify her suggestion that we should keep an ideal standard of goodness in mind, Murdoch directs us to the New Testament advice of Paul in his Letter to the Philippians:

> Whatsoever things are true, whatsoever things are honest, whatsoever things are just, whatsoever things

are pure, whatsoever things are lovely, whatsoever
things are of good report; if there be any virtue, and
if there be any praise, think on these things.

Pondering an 'ideal goodness' will sometimes help us through
the minefield of moral choice: we don't have to define that
ideal precisely, but the more we concentrate on things we
recognise as being 'good', the more easily we will be able
to act in harmony with our imagined ideal. An apparently
intuitive understanding of right and wrong will usually not
be intuitive at all: it will be the result of much trial and error,
much thought, and much practice.

Keeping company with people we regard as good people;
reading books and seeing films that give us some insight
into the dynamics of human behaviour and its links to good
and bad outcomes; reflecting on our own experiences in the
light of an ideal of goodness . . . such exercises or disciplines
give us practice in recognising what is right and wrong for
us. We can be inspired by those who have demonstrated
what goodness-in-action looks like and we can be encouraged by people who are ahead of us on the same journey.
The ability to decide what's right and wrong may never
come automatically, given the complexity of lives lived in
ever-changing circumstances, which is why we need to
develop the art of moral mindfulness.

Murdoch's idea of the 'love of the Good' can be combined
with more pragmatic, utilitarian considerations: moral

mindfulness demands that we explore both approaches, always asking *two* fundamental questions of ourselves:

- Is this action in harmony with my ideal of virtuous behaviour?
- Will this action cause more good than harm; more harmony than discord?

The German philosopher Martin Heidegger offers us a metaphor that reminds us of the need to ask *both* those sets of questions. In an autobiographical essay, *Der Feldweg*, written in 1949, Heidegger describes the experience of walking along a path on the outskirts of the town where he had grown up, and coming upon an oak tree on the edge of the woods. Struck (in the way philosophers sometimes are) by the way the tree was both rooted to the earth and open to the sky, Heidegger was moved to write this:

> Everything real and true only prospers if mankind fulfils at the same time the two conditions of being ready for the demands of highest heaven and of being safe in the shelter of the fruitful earth.

That's a poetic way of putting it, and it reflects a somewhat religious shift in Heidegger's thinking at the time. (By the way, if you need reminding about the frailty of human nature and the inconsistencies that plague many of our attempts to define our moral principles, ponder this: Heidegger, who was capable of writing so beautifully and thoughtfully about the human condition, was at one time a Nazi. The capacity to think clearly about moral issues did not prevent him from supporting, at an earlier stage of his life, views and values many, including the older Heidegger, would regard as unsupportable.)

The picture of the oak—rooted to the earth and open to the sky—vividly illustrates the necessary connection between the utilitarian and the idealist approaches to the achievement of moral clarity. One without the other is like the oak either without its roots or without its branches.

Utilitarian questions remind us that we are 'rooted to the earth'—that is, embedded in a community. Our roots connect us to our social context and we depend on that context to sustain and nurture our emotional health as well as our moral health. Therefore we have a moral responsibility to consider ways in which our actions might affect the quality of those connections. These are the questions about *consequences for others* that we explored in Chapter 2: will this action cause more good than harm? Will it cause more pleasure than pain? Will it produce the greatest possible good for the greatest possible number of people? Will it cause *any* harm?

Strict utilitarians might try to tell you that such questions are enough, but questions about consequences for others will not necessarily clarify what's right or wrong for us in every situation. It's easy to imagine an action that has no negative consequences for other people but still makes us feel uneasy—as if it's wrong in some way that is different from the strictly utilitarian sense of 'wrong'. You might be involved in developing a business strategy that breaks no laws but seems to you to be morally dubious—perhaps because it represents values that are in conflict with your own.

Equally, we can imagine feeling that something is right for us to do, even if it doesn't immediately add to the sum of human happiness. Terminating a three-cornered love affair might come into this category. You might have managed to convince yourself that the third person in the triangle—your lover's spouse, for instance—is not being harmed by your relationship, and it may seem 'wrong' in some sense for you to sacrifice the intense personal happiness you have been experiencing. You might even be forced to acknowledge that leaving the relationship may cause pain and distress to the lover you are leaving, and yet you might feel that, because of your desire to live in harmony with a particular idea of virtue, leaving is the right course of action for you.

Whistleblowers are sometimes made to feel as if they are making too much fuss over a matter of principle, when no one is being harmed and no obvious good may be achieved by the exposure of someone else's unethical behaviour. Yet they go ahead because their consciences demand that they should.

Secret acts of charity are often about being 'open to the sky' as well as 'rooted to the earth': though they may contribute to other people's comfort, happiness or well-being, a powerful additional motive might be the conviction that we are serving our own sense of personal integrity. Some of the sacrifices parents make on behalf of their children, similarly, might be as much about the parents' wish to approach an ideal of 'good parenting' as about the actual welfare of the child in a specific situation.

Such examples remind us that a healthy oak is not only rooted to the earth but also open to the sky: there are ideals like truth, purity, compassion, tolerance, goodness or humility that call on us to consider something more than the merely utilitarian effects of our actions on others and encourage us to do the right thing for its own sake.

Visualisation

As Iris Murdoch says, we can 'grow by looking' but we can also grow by *thinking* about the consequences of our actions, and by *imagining* how things might be made better or worse by the actions we take or refrain from taking. It can be fun to explore, to imagine, to speculate about all the possible consequences—wonderful and dreadful—that might flow from our actions. Morality is, after all, the work of the imagination. Making moral choices is a creative act and, like all creative acts, it requires courage and involves risk.

Suppose we are confronted with a moral dilemma in which two different courses of action are open to us.

Will we withhold medical treatment from an elderly, terminally ill patient, or maintain it?

Will we tell a potential buyer everything we know about the condition of a house, or avoid mentioning some problem with the plumbing that would not become obvious until you had lived in the house for a while?

Will we reveal precisely the same information to all the parties to a business deal, or not?

Will we terminate this relationship, or not?

Will we tell a calculated lie to secure an advantage for one of our children, or not?

Will we take revenge on someone who has wronged us, or not?

Will we blow the whistle on the unethical actions of a superior at work and risk being fired, or keep quiet and regard the matter as being the personal responsibility of that other person?

Will we make a significant donation to a charity that attends to the needs of the poor and homeless, or save that money in case of some emergency in the family?

We can stimulate moral mindfulness by visualising ourselves acting in *both* scenarios—following each course of action in turn and then trying to visualise the impact of each outcome on all concerned. It's a bit like creating two different stories about the same situation, casting yourself as the central character in each version and then seeing how the story unfolds. If the situation is sufficiently serious, and you're uncertain about what is the right thing to do, it may be helpful to write the stories down: this is what I visualise happening if I follow plan A; this is what I visualise happening if I follow plan B.

Tell both stories as fully as you can, being as honest as possible with yourself. Once you have fully immersed yourself in the process, imagine yourself following each course of action to its probable conclusion, then ask yourself such questions as these:

- Now that I've fully explored the likely outcomes of the two scenarios, do I find myself admiring the central character in one version more than the other? Does one central character seem better or worse, as a moral being, than the other?
- If I follow one course of action rather than the other, how am I likely to feel in the future? (In both scenarios, imagine yourself one year or even five years hence, looking back at this situation and the way you handled it.)
- Were the consequences of one course of action easier to imagine than the consequences of the other? (Are you hiding something from yourself?)
- In these two stories, was anyone hurt or offended or disadvantaged by either course of action? Now I have visualised it as if it had really happened, can I see any way I could have avoided that harm?
- Whose well-being was affected, positively or negatively, by my actions? In each scenario, who is clearly better off or worse off—my spouse or partner, my children, my parents, my friends, my workmates, business associates or professional colleagues . . . or myself? Were any innocent bystanders affected?

- Does it feel as if my actions were harder to justify in one case than the other?
- If both these stories were acted out on stage or screen, would I be more comfortable being publicly identified as the central character in one case than the other?

The person who masters the art of *visualisation* is well on the way to developing the habit of moral mindfulness.

And yet...

When we've asked the utilitarian *and* the idealist questions, and when we've visualised all the possible outcomes of the various courses of action open to us, will we have achieved the moral clarity and confidence we yearn for? Does moral mindfulness guarantee that we'll get it right, every time?

Unhappily, no. We are still human—frail, messy, irrational, and liable to be swept by passions that can blow us off course. We are still capable of deciding to do one thing and yet doing another: 'I knew it was the wrong thing to do, but I just couldn't help myself.' And we will sometimes find ourselves in situations where we have to choose the lesser of two evils.

But perhaps we should draw encouragement from Cambridge University's Professor of Philosophy, Simon Blackburn, in *Being Good*:

If we are careful, and mature, and imaginative, and fair, and nice, and lucky, the moral mirror in which

108

we gaze at ourselves may not show us saints. But it need not show us monsters, either.

That may strike you as a modest aim, but it is a realistic reminder of the fact that even when we are doing our best to 'be good', we may fall short of our own standards. That's no cause for despair, but simply a reminder that we live in an imperfect and unpredictable world, which is the very reason why it is vital for people of goodwill to pursue their dreams of a virtuous life.

8

The only life you can control is your own

Moral mindfulness is a very different thing from moralising. One is concerned with our inner state—our own responses to the moral dilemmas that confront us. The other is about trying to influence other people to conform to some ideal we have in mind for them, or to change them in ways we think will make them more acceptable to us: more responsible, more sensitive, or perhaps more obedient to a code of ethics we ourselves subscribe to and would like them to adopt.

While there is nothing wrong with discussing other people's moral dilemmas with them, especially if they invite you to do so, there is a huge difference between helping people work out their own destiny and attempting to prescribe their destiny for them.

When you find yourself trying to influence someone to conform to your moral standards, you might do well to remind yourself of two strong grounds for desisting. The first is itself a moral objection: moralising, when it takes the form of an attempt to reconstruct someone else's moral framework, represents an invasion of their right to be whoever they want to be. The second is a more harshly practical reason: moralising rarely works. Attempts to change other people's moral outlook are usually stressful for both parties, create bad feeling and, in the process, reinforce the very position you're trying to change.

When people feel their attitudes or behaviour are under attack, the most natural thing for them to do is defend themselves, and the act of defending ourselves almost always has a reinforcing effect. This is why religious, ethnic or other minorities tend to draw strength from persecution: they cling even more staunchly to the beliefs their persecutors are attacking. Attacks on other people's value systems aren't merely unproductive; they are usually counter-productive.

Assuming most of us are serious when we say we'd like to live with less stress, it's surprising that we pay so little attention to what may be the biggest single step we can take in the direction of stress-reduction. As usual with such things, it's easy to state and difficult to put into practice: in your personal relationships, the best way to relieve stress is to *stop trying to change people*.

(Perhaps you caught the whiff of a paradox . . . you thought I was trying to influence you to stop trying to influence people? Not at all; I'm merely offering you a choice.

You are absolutely free to do as you please, of course, and to accept whatever consequences flow from that.)

Unquestionably, one of the biggest sources of stress in our lives is the stress arising from the almost irresistible urge to change the way other people think and act, so they'll conform more closely to the way we'd like them to think and act. Yes, it's frustrating to stand by while someone does something unwise, unhelpful or, in your opinion, unethical, especially if you think you know better. ('How could you *do* such a thing?') But there's something even more frustrating than that: watching your attempts at persuasion produce exactly the opposite effect from the one you intended.

There are plenty of healthy ways of dealing with our differences over ethical issues. We can agree to disagree, negotiate a compromise, assert ourselves, or walk away. Those are all less stressful strategies than trying to twist other people into shapes that please us.

In certain highly-charged situations, especially in the workplace, we may need to 'blow the whistle' to expose someone else's unethical practices because they are impinging on the integrity of the organisation or running the risk of bringing other people into disrepute. Generally speaking, fairness demands that such people should be advised of our intention to expose them, so they have an opportunity to right their own wrongs or admit their moral lapses to the appropriate person in authority. The fact that you intend to assuage your own conscience by exposing what you regard as their unethical behaviour is information they need to be able to take into account in deciding on their own course of action.

We are as we are; other people are as they are. That doesn't mean all our natures are predetermined in some cosmic almanac. Our circumstances create formative influences that interact with our genetic make-up. We change and adapt all the time; that's what life is. And we do, of course, influence each other by example or even by explanations of why we do things the way we do. (Explaining your *own* position is a very different thing from moralising.) The problem arises when we try to intervene in that process by putting pressure on other people to conform to *our* ideal.

Unless they are already disposed to make changes in response to the whispers of their own consciences, and unless they have asked us for our guidance, expecting them to change merely in response to our demands that they should is about as futile as unrequited love, or as pointless as trying to teach children something they're not ready, willing and able to learn. My mother once remarked that she felt as if she had merely watched her children grow up, with little discernible effect on their development. She was both right and wrong: like all parents, her influence was mainly through example, rather than hectoring. (Leave the hectoring to those with a commercial or political agenda. Even among the slick professionals, though, the failure rate is high: over 80 per cent of new products fail, and when were you last persuaded to change your vote by an election campaign advertisement?)

Occasionally, you come across victims of persuasion: a husband, perhaps, nagged into submission by a wife who, having got him where she wants him, loses her respect for the remnant of a man she once loved. 'Aisle altar hymn,' runs the old joke about the bride's choice of wedding music.

But are we ever really altered by such relentless pressure? Aren't people more likely to develop, deep inside, a volcanic resentment that will eventually erupt? Or the opposite: mightn't the nagged and needled heart coat itself in emotional permafrost, becoming impervious to even the mildest attempt at 'correction' or 'improvement'?

If you ask someone to change and they don't, the message is obvious. Why not accept it and lower your stress level? Life lived as a contest of wills diminishes both of you. If you are operating according to different value systems, your moral injunctions are almost certain to fall on deaf ears—unless the other person is deliberately trying to goad you, in which case your every sigh of frustration, your every frown of disapproval, your every little tantrum will be like a trophy.

You can control your response to other people

Trying to change someone is the ultimate put-down, no matter how much we might try to justify the attempt by claiming to be acting in the best interests of the other person, 'saving them from themselves', or instructing them in matters on which they appear to be in need of instruction (even if they don't seem to realise it themselves). But when we exert moral pressure on another person, this is tantamount to saying: 'You're an unsatisfactory person, but you're in luck—I know how to fix you up.' Another person's behaviour might seem infuriating, frustrating and puzzling to you, but that's how they behave and, mostly, that will be how they choose to behave.

If you have recognised that you're unlikely to change them, but you still want to maintain a relationship with them, there's only one realistic possibility: you'll need to change your own response to the way they are, and the things they do. Indeed, the only thing you *can* control in that situation is your own response.

Of course, you are at liberty to express your disapproval, bewilderment, disappointment or even anger in the face of behaviour that offends you. It is perfectly reasonable to state your *own* preferences in a particular matter, and even to describe how you might choose to handle the situation differently. Those messages can be received with relatively little pain, because they are messages about you, not the other person.

When my husband's mother was dying, I was frankly appalled at the way he handled it. When it was obvious she was close to the end, he went away on a skiing trip he'd had planned for ages. He said there was nothing more he could do, and his mother might linger on for weeks. I thought that was wrong, and I told him so. He said I could handle my own mother's death any way I liked, when the time came, which I thought was heartless. But he was right, in a way. It was none of my business how he chose to handle those last few days of his mother's life. I didn't really know what was going on in his head; people have to deal with bereavement and grief in their own way. It wasn't much help, me trying to tell him what he should do, or even expressing my strong disapproval of the way he was handling the situation. I sometimes feel as if I'm expressing the emotions for both of us, but I don't think I get any credit for that, and why should I? I only end up putting pressure on him.

What about children?

It almost goes without saying that there are special circumstances in which we are obliged to exert direct influence over another person's moral behaviour—for example, in the case of young children and people with severely limited intellectual resources. Yet, in such cases, the term 'moral behaviour' may scarcely apply. When people are unable to exercise moral discernment because of their immaturity or limited cognitive capacity, those responsible for their care and well-being must make such decisions on their behalf.

In the case of children over the age of about four, however, it is generally unhelpful for parents to lay down the law and impose rules designed to ensure blind obedience. Even at that tender age, it's time to begin the long process of teaching children what moral sensitivity entails. Young children are entitled to know *why* the rules are as they are; they should be encouraged to recognise the rights and needs of others— starting with their parents and siblings, but soon extending to neighbours, schoolmates, teachers and other children and adults they come into contact with as their circle widens. Although they may be incapable of fine moral judgments until well into adulthood, they can at least be made aware, from the very beginning of the learning process, that actions have consequences.

Studies of early childhood development suggest that most children have acquired a reasonably clear idea of 'fairness' by the age of about four; by that stage, most children have also grasped the notion of 'sharing', so the process of moral formation is well under way. There is still a very long way to go, of course: many young children who *understand* 'sharing' still don't want to share, and not all those who know what 'fair' *means* are prepared to act fairly—especially if they can see themselves being disadvantaged as a result. Life still has many painful lessons to teach them!

The process of moral formation is part of the natural process of socialisation, but it is slow. Although some four- and five-year-olds can already hear the whispers of their embryonic consciences, children cannot be expected to make complex moral judgments, especially those that might contradict their appetites for fun, food and friends. (Neither can many teenagers, by the way, but why stop there? Many adults can't either.) Parents probably need more patience in giving their children moral guidance than in any other area of parenting, because it is so tempting to impose yet more rules rather than explaining the rights and wrongs of particular situations, case by case.

Right through their teenage years, and even into early adulthood, most people experience an inner struggle between self-indulgence and self-control. Finding the point of balance is an important part of maturation, but it doesn't generally happen until many mistakes have been made. Sympathetic discussion of moral choices that have turned out badly can be useful stepping-stones on the journey towards moral clarity; every airing of a moral issue is a contribution to the child's ultimate development of the habit of moral mindfulness. For a parent, one of the most surprising yet potentially satisfying experiences is the discovery that your child is beginning to make some independent moral decisions—even if they are different from the ones you might want them to make.

9

Guilt, shame and forgiveness

Guilt gets a lot of bad press these days. According to the modern view, we should try to conquer our feelings of guilt; rise above them; consign them to outer darkness where negative, destructive emotions belong. 'Guilt is like cancer: don't let it eat away at your self-esteem! Never admit your guilt! Never apologise!'

In fact, guilt is an authentic human emotion that does important work for us—not only ringing alarm bells that alert us to our own moral lapses, but also reassuring us that our conscience is in good working order.

Guilt and shame are close relatives, but there is a difference. Shame is what we feel when we know we have disappointed *other people* by our behaviour; guilt is what we feel when we have offended against *our own* moral code. Shame is generally associated with feelings of social humiliation; guilt is typically associated with a more personal sense of failure.

Of course, the two can occur simultaneously and we often try to deal with them in similar ways. Usually, we will need to make some kind of confession of our misdemeanour (preferably to the person we have offended, disappointed or wronged, but in certain circumstances to a priest or some other person in whom we have invested the authority to forgive us): 'I feel really embarrassed about what I did. I'm sorry to have disappointed you and I'll try not to do it again.'

Sometimes we make compensatory gestures that we hope will redeem us in the eyes of those we have offended or disappointed—as if to say, 'See, I'm not so bad, after all.' We may pay for a repair, or buy a gift, or offer to do something practical to help the person we have wronged. Sometimes this is welcome; sometimes offensive. We must assess each situation carefully. But, ultimately, we must endure our shame and work through it, admitting it, and seeking understanding and forgiveness.

Where guilt is involved, an apology is the usual trigger for forgiveness, and, conversely, forgiveness is the usual trigger for the expiation of guilt. Some form of reparation is often necessary, as well. We must do whatever is necessary in order to secure the forgiveness of the person we have wronged. But once we have been forgiven, it's time to let the guilt dissipate. We should learn from it, be chastened by it, acknowledge that it is an appropriate emotion in the circumstances . . . and then let it go. Like all intense emotions, guilt and shame recede over time, unless there are constant reminders, or a lack of forgiveness by the person we have offended. But for most of us, in most circumstances, guilt and shame are relatively transient experiences: they do their work for us, then leave us alone.

Of course, there is such a thing as neurotic guilt that refuses to dissipate and persists beyond its 'use by' date. You can pick it: it's the kind of guilt you'd be embarrassed to describe to someone, because you know they would think you were being irrational or unreasonable for 'nursing' it for so long. It's the kind of guilt you seem unable to let go, long after the event, even when you've confessed your wrongdoing and been forgiven by the party you've offended. Such guilt is often blurred with regret: it's natural to experience long-term regret about having done something we now think of as unwise, but to attach guilt to regret is to give it unwarranted power over us.

If neurotic guilt is interfering with your ability to get on with your life, you may need to reassure yourself that you have, indeed, been forgiven. If the forgiveness you crave isn't forthcoming, then, sooner or later, you'll have to let that problem go, too, and find a way of forgiving yourself. In either case, you may need some specific, short-term counselling to help you over the hump of your lingering guilt.

Some guilt is inappropriate—either because it springs from the remarkably common habit of always assuming we're in the wrong, even when we're not; because we have been conditioned to accept blame when other people try to dish it out; because someone has withheld forgiveness from us; or perhaps because we haven't yet found a way to forgive ourselves.

There is no need to be afraid of authentic and reasonable guilt: listen to it, respond to its message, look where it is pointing and then decide whether it is a genuine wake-up call or the result of some old conditioning you should try to shake off.

Projecting our own guilt onto others

Once we become alert to the difference between authentic, appropriate guilt and neurotic or inappropriate guilt, we may also find cases where, instead of dealing with appropriate guilt, we have transferred it to someone else—convincing ourselves that *they* should feel guilty—through the clever psychological defence mechanism of projection.

'Projection' was a term introduced to psychology by Freud. It refers to the process of defending ourselves against a motive or emotion within us by denying it in ourselves and attributing it to someone else. For example, we may fail to deal with our own anger by perceiving it in other people (often going so far as to criticise them harshly for 'their' anger).

Projection explains why we are so ready to detect in other people the very faults and shortcomings we manage to ignore in ourselves. We might disown our guilt or shame over our destructive feelings of jealousy by accusing others of being excessively jealous; we might deny our tendency to enjoy gossip by criticising others as shameless gossips. Here's a modern description of projection at work, taken from Colin C. Tipping's *Radical Forgiveness*: 'If you want to know what you dislike about yourself and have largely disowned, simply look at what annoys you about the people who come into your life. Look into the mirror they provide.' Tipping argues that the presence of a lot of apparently angry people in your life probably means you haven't dealt with some anger of your own. If people seem to withhold love from you, you might yourself be unwilling to love.

Similarly, if you find it hard to accept criticism, or feel as if you are surrounded by people who are critical of you, that may be because you are too free in your criticism of others.

More controversially, Tipping suggests that because we project our own weaknesses or unresolved guilt onto others, seeing our own reflection in them, we can 'clear' our original pain by forgiving the person onto whom we have projected our own problem. Since that's where it has gone, that's where we have to deal with it. Others might say we should first take the guilt back—accept that the problem is ours and even seek the forgiveness of the person we have unjustifiably attacked—and then deal with it *in us*. Whichever destination we choose, the journey is the same: forgiveness is the key to the expiation of guilt.

The power of forgiveness

Forgiveness is a liberating, healing experience for the forgiver and the forgiven. One of the most generous acts we ever perform, forgiveness doesn't only clear the way for another person's guilt to be resolved; it also enables us to see that other people can be valued and accepted with all their short-comings and frailties. We forgive people not because we think they are 'not really like that', but because we know they *are* really like that *and* we forgive them. Indeed, that's *why* we need to forgive them.

Unless you are a saint, your willingness to forgive someone who has wronged you, or slighted you, or offended you will serve as a reminder that we are all capable of such behaviour; we all disappoint each other sometimes; we are all in need of forgiveness for the darkness of our thoughts or the murkiness of our motives, even if our actions seem acceptable on the surface.

Forgiveness is a crucial part of understanding the nature of the human condition, as well as understanding this person who has wronged you in some particular case. Once you *understand*, forgiveness becomes possible. As long as you are resistant to understanding—remaining defensive, outraged, offended, aloof, critical, resentful—forgiveness will be hard to offer because the gulf will be too wide to bridge. We can't will ourselves to 'forgive and forget', but we can forgive and then live as if we have truly forgiven.

The most liberating form of forgiveness, often hardest to achieve, is our forgiveness of ourselves. Many people who harbour inappropriate or neurotic guilt do so because they have not understood themselves sufficiently to be able to forgive themselves. It's not uncommon to come across people labouring under a burden of heavy guilt who say that although the person they wronged has long since forgiven them, they still can't forgive themselves.

What that really means is that they haven't yet fully entered into the *process* of forgiveness: once you accept that you've done what you've done, felt the contrition appropriate to the deed, apologised and been forgiven by the person you've wronged, it's time to forgive yourself and *move on*. Again, this doesn't mean we'll be able to forget what we've done, any more than we can quickly or easily forget something unpleasant or wrong that someone else has done to us. Forgiveness is not about forgetting; it's about moving on.

Forgiving ourselves is not a simple case of letting ourselves off the hook. It is not a matter to be taken lightly or impatiently. But as the final link in this chain of events, it makes perfect sense to seek our own forgiveness: after all, we have let *ourselves* down by our bad behaviour; it is our own moral code we have breached.

'Can one forgive oneself?' asks André Comte-Sponville. 'Of course, since one can hate oneself and overcome self-hatred. What hope would there be for wisdom otherwise? Or for happiness? Or for peace?'

Self-forgiveness is one of the most significant manifestations of moral mindfulness: we have reflected on the wrongness of our actions, we have sought the forgiveness of the person we have wronged, perhaps we have made some restitution and now . . . the final hurdle: we must let our guilt go by forgiving ourselves—deliberately, thoughtfully and with appropriate contrition.

In the same way as our forgiveness of others is based on our recognition and acceptance of their frailties and flaws, so our forgiveness of ourselves is an act of humility, not pride. Forgiving ourselves and each other doesn't make us perfect; it only sets us free. We do not wipe the slate clean: we learn to accept (and even love) the dirty slate.

The English poet Alexander Pope (1688–1744) famously wrote: 'To err is human; to forgive, divine.' Religious believers may say that, in the end, only God can forgive. But those who believe there is a divine spark in all of us would say that our capacity to forgive ourselves is the greatest work of the 'God within': that is, we can act in a godly way not only by forgiving others but by forgiving ourselves, as well.

However we characterise it, and whatever disciplines we develop for achieving it, self-forgiveness is an essential weapon in the fight against neurotic, self-crippling guilt. It is an act of 'closure' for a person who has been through the cycle of wrong action–guilt–apology–forgiveness. For completion of the cycle, we must acknowledge *to ourselves* all that has happened, fully admit *to ourselves* our part in it, then forgive ourselves and move on—determined, of course, never to repeat that mistake.

PART TWO

PUTTING MORAL MINDFULNESS TO WORK

10

Does the end ever justify the means?

W riting in the *Sydney Morning Herald* at the time, Geoff Kitney raised an important moral issue regarding Australia's participation in the US-led 2003 invasion of Iraq:

They could be two different wars, the one John Howard sent the troops off to and the one he is now welcoming them home from. The war the troops went to was a war to strip Saddam Hussein of his weapons of mass destruction and to prevent him giving his terrorist brothers in the Al-Qaeda organisation access to these stockpiles.

The war they are coming home from is a war of liberation, a war which freed the oppressed Iraqi people from the yoke of Saddam's brutal and murderous regime and offers the hope of freedom and democracy taking root in the Middle East.

Australians obviously prefer the war the troops are coming home from. The polls that showed, before war in Iraq was declared, deep misgivings in the community about the involvement of Australian troops now show great pride over the role the troops played.

From the very start, Australia's participation in the invasion of Iraq was mired in moral controversy. The prime minister's decision to commit Australian troops to the conflict, without United Nations backing, was presumably based on his belief that if the war were won and Saddam's weapons of mass destruction uncovered, many opponents of the war would be converted into supporters, perhaps on the grounds that 'the end justifies the means'. When no weapons of mass destruction turned up, a different 'end' had to be found to justify the invasion—hence the talk of 'liberation'.

When we are tempted to accept that the end justifies the means—that actions regarded as morally undesirable in themselves can become 'right' because they achieve a morally desirable outcome—we'll find ourselves in pretty rough company. That is precisely the justification used by torturers who inflict awful pain on their victims in order to extract confessions of wrongdoing, or other information that will serve the cause of the torturer.

It's also the justification for bribery: we might regard bribery itself as morally repugnant, but what if it achieves an objective we approve of? What if bribery succeeds in producing compliant children, for instance? Does that make it an acceptable strategy in child-raising? What if bribery encourages criminals to give up valuable information that leads to the successful prosecution of their partners in crime? There's a fine line here, of course: under pressure, what parent hasn't yielded to bribery for some short-term peace? And isn't plea-bargaining in criminal trials just a legitimised form of bribery?

The temptation to employ bribery presents us with an interesting moral dilemma. We might occasionally decide that even though bribery is wrong, we are prepared to use it in circumstances where there seems to be no other way of achieving an outcome that's important to us, or where the bribery itself seems like the lesser of two evils—the other 'evil' being, say, a child's bad behaviour, or criminals getting away with their crimes. There'll be other factors to take into account, though, especially when we're dealing with children: 'Is this a rare event, or is it becoming a habit? Will my example teach the child a lesson I would rather not teach? Will it imply a set of values I don't actually admire?'

Although proper reflection may sometimes lead us into soft applications of the proposition that 'the end justifies the means', it's perhaps wise to regard this as a slippery slope we'd do well to avoid. Once you've justified one morally dubious action by reference to some morally attractive 'end', it will become easier to convince yourself, in future, that this is an argument that can be made to work. It is, after all, one of the most seductive of all moral arguments: this might not be, of itself, a good thing to do, but look at the good result it will achieve!

War is the most dramatic example of the argument, but there are many others. The Australian government's treatment of asylum-seekers who arrive by boat (sometimes unfairly described as 'illegal immigrants') is a classic case. The argument runs like this: we'll hold these people in offshore detention centres and treat them more harshly and less humanely than we treat the criminals in our prisons—and we will even detain small children—because this will discourage other people seeking asylum from trying to come here by boat. When the trickle of asylum-seekers arriving by boat did eventually dry up, a succession of prime ministers and immigration ministers claimed that this end had fully justified the means used to achieve it. Australia's treatment of asylum-seekers in detention centres has become the subject of increasing disquiet in the Australian community, amid trenchant criticism from the United Nations and disturbing claims about the treatment of detainees made by doctors and psychologists who have visited the centres. And yet, in the eyes of these ministers, all this counted for nothing compared with the achievement of a political objective.

Is winning everything?

Sport is another showcase for the dodgy logic that says ends can justify means. Australians take great pride in what they regard as the disproportionately strong representation of Australians in the top echelons of world sport—cricket, netball, tennis, swimming, golf, rugby, hockey, rowing—but how far are we prepared to go in the pursuit of victory? Is a win-at-all-costs philosophy morally sustainable? How much money are we prepared to spend on the training of young athletes at places like the Institute of Sport? (The answer is: far more, per capita, than we spend on the training of doctors, scientists, musicians or philosophers; so there's presumably something about the symbolism of competitive sport that deeply appeals to us.)

But what do we get for our money, apart from winners? When we take young athletes and impose a ruthless training regimen on them, honing their skills and fuelling their competitive urges, should we expect them to emerge as well-rounded human beings, full of joie de vivre, imbued with love for their fellows, passionate about fair play and with a realistic appreciation of the place of sport in a balanced life? Isn't there a risk—and isn't it a *moral* risk?—that they might emerge, instead, as rather driven individuals with some unattractive, unhealthy attitudes arising from the encouragement of the idea that winning is everything? When your sense of self-worth is tied to your performance—whether you're an athlete or a money-market trader—dark and damaging neuroses lurk.

Do we believe that the commercialisation of sport improves its moral tone, or does 'big' money tend to make it a more ruthless affair, in which concerns about performance-based remuneration might overshadow team loyalties or a commitment to the spirit of fair play? Are we comfortable with the elevation of athletes to elite status in a way that contradicts our widely trumpeted resistance to elitism in other areas (such as academia or the arts)?

And how do we feel about the use of performance-enhancing drugs that can't be detected by normal means? Is it all right as long as you can get away with it? Is it fair? (And what if, as some athletes claim, 'everyone's doing it'?) What about sports players who exploit the rules in ways that are legally acceptable but, like the 'professional foul' or sledging, contrary to the spirit of the game? Do we accept that any tactic that doesn't technically break the rules is fair—in other words, that the end justifies the means?

A refinement of 'the end justifies the means' can be found in the argument that if one's *intentions* are pure, this makes otherwise unethical behaviour all right. People use this argument in the political context: 'politics is a dirty game, where telling lies and doing dark deals are things you have to do in order to achieve power and, without power, you'll get nowhere.' The former Labor Party powerbroker Graham Richardson summed it up in the title of his political auto-biography: *Whatever It Takes.* In other words, the argument runs, our passionate commitment to a particular political agenda entitles us to behave in ways we might otherwise disapprove of. But at what price?

Thugs or bullies who get their way—a coveted appointment, for example, or a political victory—by manipulation, intimidation or deception will never be able to claim the moral authority they crave: they have sacrificed it through the very process of winning. No matter how well they may perform in whatever role they win for themselves, their victory has been rendered hollow by the very means they chose to achieve it. Similarly, the liar may gain some advantage through deception, but a high price will be paid in terms of the erosion of personal integrity and loss of moral authority.

Writing in the *London Review of Books* about Britain's participation in the 2003 invasion of Iraq, David Runciman recalled Disraeli's defence of the British invasion of Abyssinia in 1867 on the grounds of 'the purity of our purpose' (i.e. the freeing of nine British officials who had been taken hostage by the King of Abyssinia). Contrasting that situation with the 2003 war on Iraq, Runciman observed that the British people were angry with their prime minister, Tony Blair, for entering into the war in Iraq, and 'trumpeting the purity of his purpose, when what matters is the consequences of his actions'.

In Australia, defenders of the historical policy of removing Indigenous children from their parents and placing them with white families often resort to the same 'pure motives' argument: 'At the time, people felt they were doing the right thing—they honestly believed that policy was in the best interests of the children themselves.' Opponents of the policy find it almost impossible to accept that anyone could ever have believed it was in the best interests of Indigenous people. They argue that the ultimate consequences of such a trauma in the lives of the mothers and children were so negative—and so *likely* to be negative—as to challenge the claim that the motives for such behaviour could ever have been 'pure'.

When it is counter-argued—as it often is—that some of the children involved seemed *not* to have been traumatised by these events and, indeed, subsequently claimed to have benefited from having an upbringing in the care of white families, we are back with 'the end justifies the means'. Are we going to justify actions that seem to us to have been wrong, by saying that, in the end, things turned out well for some of those involved? Where should we draw the line? Should we say the policy was acceptable if 51 per cent of those taken were judged to have gleaned more benefit than pain from the experience? Remember that one of the possible tests to be applied in such cases is: 'Will *anyone* be harmed by this action?' 'Selective benevolence' would be a very strange moral ideal.

New York Times columnist Maureen Dowd quotes the maxim of Robert Moses, a New York builder who never let public opinion get in the way of his bulldozer: 'If the ends don't justify the means, what does?' Moses had conventional wisdom on his side. Who hasn't remarked, at some time, that 'the end justifies the means', in the context of child-rearing, management, commerce, politics or war? It sounds so plausible, so sensible, so reasonable. But to fall for it is to open the floodgates of self-interest, to accept the tyranny of 'ends', and—worst of all—to abandon the noble ideal that every action undertaken on the way to achieving a morally acceptable outcome should itself be morally acceptable.

Moral mindfulness entails moral vigilance. In spite of the seductions of worthwhile ends and good intentions (or 'pure motives') that encourage us to make moral choices we might otherwise eschew, there does seem to be a principle at stake here: we are likely to gain most clarity about the rightness or wrongness of any action—whether an end in itself or a means to an end—if we evaluate it on its own merits and decide whether it counts as 'virtuous behaviour'. Good motives and ultimate outcomes are a very shaky basis for justifying actions we would otherwise regard as being wrong. In any case, since we can never be certain of an outcome, we can't truthfully say in advance that the end justifies the means. That's something we could only ever claim with hindsight.

It's best to assume that the end *never* justifies the means. Although we may decide to compromise this principle in certain cases, we would do well to resist the idea that an occasional compromise renders the principle itself invalid.

11

Are the rules different for sex?

There's not much point in asserting that procreation is the primary purpose of sexual activity: that may be true in a narrow evolutionary sense as applied to heterosexual couples, but the vast majority of sexual encounters have no such purpose. Indeed, most occasions of sexual intercourse are specifically intended *not* to result in procreation, which is why contraception is such big business. Most heterosexual couples maintain a sexual relationship even after they have had all the children they intend to have, and often continue to have sex well beyond the female's reproductive years. People at any point on the gender/sexuality spectrum have casual encounters with sexual partners for whom they feel no particular devotion—let alone commitment—and with whom they have not the slightest inclination to share the experience of parenthood. In the absence of a partner, many people seek sexual gratification via masturbation, with no prospect of pregnancy and the creation of babies unlikely to feature in their fantasies.

Viewed rationally, sex is a most peculiar form of human behaviour: we are driven to it by powerful, natural—sometimes almost irresistible—biological urges, yet we strenuously seek to avoid the very outcome that is the 'natural' consequence of the act. This may help to explain why sexual activity has been the focus of so much moralising throughout history, and why so many people feel sex is the one area of their lives where they are most sorely tempted to abandon or modify their principles.

Sex is the subject of more thought, more desire, more intense pleasure, more disappointment, more jealousy, more guilt, more shame, more anguish, more fantasies and more jokes than any other aspect of human behaviour. Some may say that all this overheated interest in sex is unhealthy; that there's too much prurient curiosity about other people's sex lives (celebrities, sporting heroes, politicians, next-door neighbours, colleagues and even people at a different points on the gender spectrum from our own); that whatever consenting adults want to get up to in private is no one's business but their own. Why, they ask, is such a fuss made about what people do with their genitalia and who they do it with?

The answer lies deep in our biological and cultural heritage. Because sexual intercourse was once essential for breeding, and because the rearing of children is such a huge part of a parent's life, it's hardly surprising that we have learned to place a high moral value on 'pair bonding' and its moral equivalent—monogamy. Traditionally, this was based on the assumption that the female would be dependent on a male to protect and provide for her through the years of child-rearing. Perhaps inevitably, that kind of thinking led to the situation where many men came to regard their wives as possessions. The ideal of monogamy linked to female dependency is so firmly rooted in our cultural heritage that it persists today even in societies where the independence of women has robbed that ancient argument of its relevance.

Biologists suggest that the euphoria of romantic love is programmed to last for about two years. Anecdotally, two years does seem about right: it's roughly the period during which ecstatic passion can usually be sustained—though some couples would claim to have kept it alive for much longer than that and, indeed, to have made the maintenance of passion a high priority in their relationship.

The normal tendency for romantic love either to wane or to evolve into something different, but more enduring, helps to explain why people who are bonded to a mate can occasionally be attracted to a person outside that relationship. The appeal is both carnal and nostalgic. It may also explain why some people become addicted to romance: they resist being drawn into the 'trap' of a committed relationship because they know they will be inducted into a stable, long-term partnership and perhaps even into parenthood. They also know they'll be expected to relinquish the carefree joys of each new experience of falling in love. So they career through life on a series of two-year cycles.

Some things we know about sex

Our relevant hormones become active in puberty and ultimately boil up into such powerful sexual desire that most of us, in our youth, will have trouble distinguishing between lust and love. So there's a moral question, right there: should we even try? Is it better for young people to experience a range of sexual partners so they can get past the early surge of lust and become more clear-headed about the kind of person with whom they might ultimately want to share a large chunk of their adult lives and, perhaps, the experience of parenthood? Or is it better for them to live a celibate life until the 'right' partner comes along and they feel ready to make a commitment? Or is there a desirable middle course?

Society fluctuates on this question and so do young people themselves . . . and, of course, the range of individual differences on such issues is very broad. The views of parents and other authority figures evolve from generation to generation, sometimes urging young people to exercise restraint and sometimes encouraging more permissive attitudes and behaviour, but their moralising is all pretty irrelevant: young people will decide for themselves; they'll make their own mistakes; they'll gradually develop a moral framework of their own. The moral strictures of older people will sometimes seem like responsible advice that sets appropriate standards for young people to aspire to, but sometimes they will generate quite disproportionate feelings of guilt among the young (feelings which may turn out to be more damaging, in the long term, than a bit of sexual horseplay). They are unlikely, however, to cause even a temporary pause in the well-established mating habits of the human species.

We also know that at almost any stage of our lives—even when we are settled in an apparently contented partner-ship—the power of the hormonal rush can take us by surprise. Sometimes it causes trouble (though a sudden surge of passion usually feels, at the time, more like liberation, ecstasy and fulfilment than 'trouble'); sometimes it creates wistful daydreams; sometimes it brings fresh passion to an established relationship; sometimes it triggers new and fruitful partnerships; and sometimes it finds expression in creative outlets like music, poetry or art. As we get older and more mature, the pangs of lust generally become easier to withstand, but sexual desire continues to play its key role in the complex experience we call 'falling in love'—sometimes under the most unexpected and inconvenient circumstances.

Some more things we have learnt about sex

- Generally speaking, when people become involved in three-cornered relationships, pain, anguish and guilt will be the ultimate result for all concerned. (But not always: some people either adjust to a relationship based on concealment, or negotiate their way to an open accom-modation of the complexity of all three people's feelings.)
- Clandestine relationships are usually exposed—sometimes because the lovers themselves, perhaps unconsciously, desire the catalytic effect of exposure.

- A sexual relationship eroded by a loss of trust is hard to repair, and sometimes impossible. Unqualified forgiveness is the only healer.

- Jealousy generally diminishes love, though it is an understandable reaction to the perception of real or imagined unfaithful behaviour. Conversely, it sometimes sends a timely and welcome signal of devotion and commitment.

- People can usually sense when their sexual partner has lost interest in them, or developed an interest in someone else. They will sometimes go into denial and direct their anger or humiliation or disappointment into bad behaviour in other departments of their lives, becoming aggressive at work, gruff with their children, randomly flirtatious, reckless behind the wheel, etc.

- When one party in a sexual relationship seeks personal gratification, with little or no thought for the pleasure and satisfaction of the other, this will undermine the personal integrity of both partners.

- Sex is the toughest training-ground for learning how to take other people seriously. 'Casual' sex often seems more casual to one partner than the other, especially after the event.

- Deceitfulness in matters of the heart is as morally risky as deceitfulness in any other context, but the emotions involved in sexual relationships are usually more intense and the sense of betrayal more bitter than in non-sexual situations.

- Sexual relationships based on power, rather than love, will usually turn to ashes, burnt out by the attempt to reconcile the irreconcilable. Power might be, as Henry Kissinger once claimed, an aphrodisiac—at least for some emotionally inadequate people. But that's power *outside* a sexual relationship: inside a relationship, love and power don't mix. Equality is love's oxygen.

Nowhere in our lives is moral mindfulness more necessary, or harder to achieve, than in the area of sexual desire and sexual relationships. We might as well acknowledge that people will behave irrationally and irresponsibly under the influence of sexual desire and that the outcome is unpredictable. People in committed relationships will occasionally fall helplessly (and 'authentically') in love with someone else and feel that to ignore such powerful attraction would actually be wrong for them, even though they may feel that leaving the marriage would, in most respects, also be wrong. They will also sometimes feel themselves possessed by raging lust for a third party that they know, even while it is happening to them, has no future and represents no threat to their committed relationship with their partner. (No wonder it's called 'the eternal triangle'; no wonder it's been the stuff of literature, poetry and art down the ages.)

When sexual desire is running hot, the cool demands of moral mindfulness are difficult to meet. If we are to make morally responsible decisions about our sex lives, we will need to have carefully weighed up the fruits of our experience, our values and our sense of virtue as part of the continuous process of working out who we are and who we want to be, so we are not taken completely by surprise when desire beckons us. We will also need to have worked out in advance what 'tests' to apply, and which virtues are worth aspiring to in our sex lives.

It would be unrealistic to expect that a list of test questions will be fairly and honestly answered in every sexual situation in which we find ourselves. Sometimes, the very essence of a sexual encounter is its unpredictability, its secrecy and its 'illicit' nature: being clandestine gives it a piquancy that both partners welcome and enjoy. Many young people experimenting with sexual relations would expect their partners to be able to tell the difference between committed and uncommitted sex, without making it explicit: mutual exploitation sometimes seems to be an implicitly accepted part of the sexual game. Even so, in circumstances where we experience some moral tension, knowing the right questions to ask ourselves can help us make more enlightened choices and more responsible decisions.

For instance: 'Is *anyone* being harmed by this—actually or potentially? Am I using this person for my own pleasure, and not intending to give more to the relationship than is necessary to achieve that goal and, if so, have I made this clear to my partner and gained his/her agreement that this is the basis on which we are acting? Am I deceiving this person into believing I am more committed than I really am? Have I been completely open about information this person has a clear moral right to know about me (for instance, that I have a sexually transmitted disease, that I am married, that

I have a child, or that I am about to leave the country)? Are we doing this because we both want to do it, we are deceiving no one else, and we both feel our integrity is not being compromised?'

When it comes to sex, what do we regard as an acceptable interpretation of the ideal of fidelity? Do we mean being faithful to a sexual partner—i.e. having that person as an exclusive partner for as long as the relationship lasts? Or do we mean being faithful to ourselves—to our sense of what we believe in, what's right for us, what values we want to uphold?

Fidelity has as much to do with being honest with yourself as being honest with your partner—and that might involve being honest about your unmet needs, your resentments, your cooling feelings, or even your attraction to someone else. Nothing will clarify your feelings towards someone outside the relationship like the prospect of discussing those feelings with your partner.

Fidelity can also be interpreted to mean that we will always be faithful to our love for each other, even if it does wane and even if we ultimately decide to part. We can honour, forever, the authenticity and the value of that love while it existed between us; we can be faithful to our shared memories; we can give each other a binding undertaking that the love we feel *now* will never be diminished or denied by the experience of growing apart, falling in love with someone else or even getting sick of each other. We loved, once, and we will always be faithful to that truth about us.

In his *Short Treatise on the Great Virtues*, André Comte-Sponville quotes a friend, a remarried divorcée, who says that, in a sense, she is still faithful to her first husband: 'I mean to our life together, to our history, our love. I don't want to disown all that.' Treasuring a life together, even when it's over, is a form of fidelity.

Would the application of the utilitarian principle ever allow us to become sexually involved with two people at once? Could we imagine a triangular situation in which we believed we were achieving the best possible outcome for all concerned? If not, how would we resolve it to minimise the pain to ourselves as well as the other people involved?

Could we reconcile having simultaneous sexual relationships with two people with the ideal of living virtuously? The answer to that question is yours alone. All that can generally be said is that, throughout history and in different cultures, moral codes on this point have varied: monogamy is by no means mankind's only model of marriage, let alone sexual relations. Many people have managed to love more than one person at a time, while many others have found the very notion abhorrent and ridiculous.

Is it anyone else's business what we do sexually? If we already have a committed sexual partner when we are attracted to someone else, is it the business of our existing partner to know that we are contemplating an involvement with that other person? Would we expect or want to be told if the roles were reversed? Could a relationship outside an existing partnership conceivably enhance that partnership, as some people have claimed an 'affair' has done for them? Or would it be bound to be destructive by creating divided loyalties and by generating a sense of guilt arising from a promise of monogamy having been broken?

Can we imagine a situation in which we loved two people in different ways—the mature love of a companionate relationship and the more passionate love of a romantic liaison—or a situation in which we loved two people in the same way? And would we expect each of those partners to accept the existence of the other? Would we be comfortable with the idea that our own partner might choose to do the same?

How much risk are we prepared to take? If we find ourselves attracted to someone outside our existing relationship, is the appeal of the third party so strong that we are prepared to leave that relationship, or live with the risk of exposure—with its attendant risk of the relationship being diminished, redefined, or even terminated?

If we were certain that such a relationship would eventually be detected and exposed, would that change our attitude to becoming involved in it? If we're not prepared for exposure, are we prepared to eliminate that risk by resisting the appeal of the new relationship, or by insisting that it be confined to a non-sexual friendship of which our existing partner is aware and with which he or she is comfortable? (Plenty of people who feel powerfully attracted to someone outside their marriage choose to confine their response to private fantasies and out-in-the-open friendship.)

In *An Intimate History of Humanity,* Theodore Zeldin speculates about the development of a new type of relationship—*amitié amoureuse* (loving friendship)—characterised by affection and intimacy without sexual expression. How would you feel about your sexual partner having such a relationship with someone else? Is it only genital sex with someone else that threatens the integrity of an existing sexual relationship, or would you be uncomfortable about your partner entering the realm of deep but non-sexual affection, emotional intensity and psychological intimacy with a friend? Can you imagine yourself in a relationship of *amitié amoureuse* that was bound by a prohibition on sexual intimacy?

Common sense tells us that many mistakes will be made in our sexual encounters and relationships, if only because the power of the human libido is so strong and unpredictable. No matter how high-minded our attitudes to sexual morality may be, we can easily find ourselves in uncharted territory. On the evidence, you'd have to say that we are not an instinctively monogamous species and great devotion and discipline is required to keep us faithful to one partner for life.

While it often seems as if the 'rules' of sexual morality were made to be bent, many people do surrender willingly and joyfully to the bonds of monogamous love. But the power of sexual desire should never be discounted. Whether it appears in the guise of love or naked lust, people find themselves attracted to each other in unexpected ways and that's sometimes wonderful and positive, and it's sometimes painful and destructive. When it comes to desire, we need to remind ourselves that, as in all other aspects of our lives, joy and pain are both authentic parts of the total experience. If we expect only pleasure and plain sailing, we haven't begun to grasp the complex nature of the human heart.

The other moral issue with sex

Sexual desire creates a moral minefield, but so does a prurient and judgmental interest in other people's sexual activities and arrangements. Indeed, it is arguable that in terms of the total contribution to human pain and misery, inappropriate curiosity about other people's sex lives is more damaging than any of their alleged sexual misbehaviour.

For example, whole generations of young people—boys especially—have been made to feel guilty about masturbation, as if it were such an affront to the natural order as to warrant condemnation (or blindness, at the very least).

People who have fallen inconveniently but authentically and deeply in love with someone other than their partner are often subjected to merciless gossip, smear and innuendo. They are rarely given credit for the agony of moral indecision they might have suffered, or for the honesty with which they confronted their dilemma. They are unlikely to be praised for the courage of their ultimate decision either to acknowledge their changed feelings and new loyalties or to terminate their 'illicit' relationship and recommit themselves to their existing partner. All such processes are traumatic and they are rarely as reckless as they may appear to those outside the triangle.

Friends and acquaintances are often troubled by what they see, and there's no doubt that watching someone trying to sort out a painfully tangled love-life can be a challenge to our capacity for compassion and understanding. When sympathy and support are called for, it is always tempting, instead, to offer easy judgments about someone else's life decisions, or to resort to gossip that is bound to damage the reputation of the victim. Can we hold our heads up and brag about our own virtue when we engage in such calculatedly destructive behaviour? It is easy to imagine couples deciding to separate in a state of moral mindfulness; it is hard to imagine someone choosing to gossip about them in a state of moral mindfulness.

It ill becomes any flawed human beings (that's you and me) to draw attention to other people's flaws—and not just to draw attention to them, but to crow and to seem almost to be celebrating their foibles and frailties! The only certainty is that when it's our turn to stumble, to behave erratically or unconventionally, other people will be as merciless in their assessments of us as we have been of everyone else.

The problem here is an inherent lack of virtue (and if virtue is its own reward, we may presume that the opposite also holds true). Taking a prurient interest in other people's sex lives and making free with judgments upon them are such transparently malevolent actions that no one could be expected to take pride in performing them. What does it say about us, then, if we are so willing to make other people's trials, misfortunes and peccadilloes the currency of our conversation?

People who feel secure in the love of their partners are typically disposed to be generous and understanding in their attitudes to other people's difficulties. Similarly, people who feel secure in their knowledge of themselves—those who have grown beyond the need for mere self-esteem—seem almost eager to see the good in others and to take a compassionate view of human frailty. So perhaps one explanation of our propensity to engage in sexual gossip lies in our own sense of sexual insecurity, and a fear of what might happen to us if our own sexual relationships were to collapse.

As we have already seen, the thing we most resent or criticise in other people is often the very thing we have refused to acknowledge as one of our own frailties—'Takes one to know one,' say the children in the schoolyard, wisely. When we hear ourselves engaging in malicious gossip about other people's sexual behaviour, we would do well to look inside ourselves for an explanation of why we are so keen to put the boot in.

Another possible explanation of our willingness to engage in sexual gossip could be that, having put up with an unsatisfactory situation and an unfulfilling relationship for many years, we are irritated by the thought that someone else has resolved *not* to put up with it and to strive for a better life. Remarriage might well be, as George Bernard Shaw once quipped, 'the triumph of hope over experience', but so what?

Perhaps the gossips' personal reservoirs of hope have been exhausted and they seek solace by inviting us to join them in mocking those who dare to make a bid for happiness and gloating over those who fail.

Sometimes the explanation will be more straightforward than any of that: sex is an irresistibly interesting topic to most of us and stories about other people's sexual adventures and misadventures are . . . well, interesting. Many people would claim to gossip harmlessly, without actually feeling malevolent towards the people concerned. But 'harmless gossip' is a dangerous idea: however innocent we might feel our participation to be, the retailing of gossip is an inherently vicious activity, likely to be damaging to its target and therefore better avoided by anyone who aspires to a virtuous life. Gossips will sometimes say 'I meant no harm'; could they ever say, 'I meant well'?

Public and private sexual morality

We can't leave the subject of people's eagerness to judge each other's sexual behaviour without acknowledging that there are lingering signs of prejudice and intolerance in the attitudes of some heterosexuals towards members of the LGBTQIA community (lesbian, gay, bisexual, transgender, queer, intersex, asexual). The degree of that intolerance was revealed in the national debate preceding the 2017 postal survey conducted to gauge the level of public support for marriage equality. Even the reluctance of a succession of prime ministers to put the matter to a vote in the parliament—despite opinion polls having consistently shown strong community support for it—was a sign of equivocation on a subject that, for a majority of Australians, was not controversial at all.

While the majority view was clearly that the legal institution of marriage should be available to same-sex couples, exactly as it is to heterosexuals, all kinds of objections were raised, including the strangest of all—that marriage equality would somehow threaten religious freedom (and this at a time when 70 per cent of heterosexual marriages take place on non-religious premises).

But perhaps the most negative aspect of the debate leading up to the postal survey was that many members of the LGBTQIA community felt as if their sexual privacy was being invaded, with their sexuality placed under a public microscope.

In the event, 62 per cent of voters supported marriage equality in the postal survey, and that result was hailed as a victory for equity and fairness. It was also perhaps a symbolic acceptance of the fact that radical shifts are taking place in society's attitudes to gender and sexuality, with the blurring of traditional distinctions now being acknowledged as a more natural and realistic approach to the idea of gender identity. It also highlighted another culture shift: at the very time when the LGBTQIA community was pushing for access to the institution of marriage, heterosexual couples have been deserting it in larger numbers than ever before.

•

The old-fashioned convention that people's private lives should remain private—apart from the details they themselves choose to reveal—has been replaced by the belief that a public figure's private life is fair game: any information that can be gleaned—even if its veracity can't be absolutely guaranteed—should be shouted from the rooftops (or at least from the covers of gossip magazines and tabloid newspapers).

In the case of politicians, the rationalisation sometimes offered for this is that if a person's private life is judged to be murky in some way—especially sexually—this raises legitimate questions about their fitness to hold office. The opponents of US presidents Bill Clinton and Donald Trump certainly claimed to hold this view: if the man can't be trusted to be faithful to his wife/keep his hands off young women/keep his pants zipped/etc, then he shouldn't be trusted with the presidency.

Yet political biographies teem with saucy revelations that some of the world's most admired and respected leaders have been adulterers or philanderers. At the time, this was presumably either unknown to the public, or seen as irrelevant to the performance of their official duties.

Writing in the *Age* at a time when an extra-marital sexual relationship between two federal politicians was in the news, Pamela Bone said this:

> I had determined not to add to the chorus of commentators on this affair, mainly because, together

with around 85 per cent of the population, I believe that whatever consenting adults do in private is their business, or the business of their respective spouses, and no one else's.

Claiming that 'the media are as obsessed with sex as the religious Right have always been', Bone went on:

> For religious conservatives, 'morality' means sexual morality. Not long ago, charges of sexual abuse were coyly referred to as 'morals charges'. As if theft or corrupt business practices did not involve morals.
>
> For those media commentators who worry about the conflict of interest involved when two politicians working on policy together are having a sexual relationship, is this the only conflict of interest? Take the sex out of it. Doesn't the fact that you like or dislike someone, that you share or don't share their religion or their politics or their general world view, influence the way you work with them? . . . The trouble is, if you take the sex out of it, there is no story.

In fact, that story sank quickly amid a general feeling that it was not relevant to the public life of either politician and was certainly not 'in the public interest' as that term is generally understood—whether or not the public were fleetingly and pruriently interested. Pamela Bone also argued that there are far more serious examples of private morality affecting public policy than those involving sex:

> Indeed, the private morality of some individuals sometimes imposes policies that affect everyone. For example, the private morality of just one man, Brian Harradine, who at one time held the balance of power in the Senate, prevented all Australian women from having access to the 'morning after' contraceptive pill, RU486 . . . The private morality of US President George Bush is likely to lead to the deaths of thousands of women in the Third World from unsafe abortions, as a result of US funding having been stopped to the United Population Fund or any other family planning organisations that offer counselling about abortion as part of their services.

And, as discussed in the Prologue, as many questions could be raised about public figures' 'income tax morality' as about their sexual morality.

Nevertheless, our obsession with the sexual aspect of private morality continues unabated, and the question is important: does a lack of honesty or fidelity in private sexual matters automatically render someone unfit to hold public office? Does a private sexual indiscretion make a public figure untrustworthy? If we were to agree with that proposition, wouldn't we also be obliged to agree that if any of us have ever behaved dishonestly or faithlessly in *any* department of our lives, we couldn't be trusted at all? If we were to adopt a view as black and white as that, personal trust would collapse.

In any case, even those who regard monogamy as a virtue would be unlikely to elevate it to the status of the *highest* virtue, given the biological evidence. Fidelity, maybe; but, as we have seen, that's a different story.

12

The rights and wrongs of leaving a relationship

It's easy to fall in love, but not so easy to stay there.

Even when the first flush of romantic love deepens and matures into something less urgent and apparently more comfortable and stable, it doesn't always endure. When the going gets too tough, the inevitable question comes up: 'To stay or not to stay?' For some people, the history of a relationship generates its own moral force: 'We've been together for so long—it would be wrong to throw all that away.' Others will argue that the length of a relationship is irrelevant to its present value: 'We ran out of steam long ago—there wasn't any point in sticking together just for the sake of our history. We both wanted to have the chance of finding a more satisfying relationship with someone else. It was time to say goodbye as partners, even though we've managed to stay friends.'

When a person decides to leave a relationship—especially if this is not a mutual decision arrived at by a process of consultation—that decision will often carry the weight of many moral questions. 'Am I leaving for the reasons I say I'm leaving? Have I concealed the existence of another lover? Am I dissatisfied with the way I'm living my own life, and attaching criticism and blame to my partner as a way of avoiding some unpalatable truths about myself? Or have I made a huge mistake which I owe it to myself and my partner to correct, by leaving as quickly and painlessly as possible? Have we grown apart, and if this is obvious to me, is it equally obvious to my partner? Am I too lazy—or too proud—to work on the issues that have caused tension between us, believing that a fresh start with someone else—or even with no one else—will be easier than trying to repair the damage? Am I assuming things are worse than they really are—dreaming, perhaps, of a freedom that may not bring me the happiness I crave? Have I overlooked the possibility that there may be deep satisfaction to be found in contributing to another's wellbeing as well as my own?'

Caitlin Thomas, the widow of Welsh poet Dylan Thomas, wrote in her autobiography, *Leftover Life to Kill*, that while she was married to Dylan, she could only think of herself as the poet's wife—an identity she bitterly resented: 'I could wholeheartedly revile my fate and say I was meant for better things' but once she was alone: 'What do I do but complain about my lack of chains'.

Decisions about terminating relationships are by no means always 'moral' decisions. Sometimes, people who thought they were well suited to each other discover that this is no longer so and agree to part—perhaps with some sadness, but with no acrimony. If there are no children involved, and the separation is managed in a way that leaves both partners feeling that they have been fairly treated (for example, about the way the split is being explained to the couple's families and friends, or about the division of property), it would be hard to generate much of a moral argument in favour of them staying together. Why should we introduce notions of 'right' and 'wrong' into an apparently straightforward arrangement that suits both parties?

At the other end of the spectrum, there appear to be equally clear-cut cases where one partner is so outraged, disgusted or disappointed by the behaviour of the other that 'I never want to see you again' can be said with complete integrity and sincerity. Moral issues may well have arisen in reaching that point, many arguments may have taken place and counselling may even have been sought, but the actual decision to terminate the relationship doesn't seem at all complicated to the person who is making it. In fact, the morality of it has become irrelevant to the emotional imperative that drives it: 'It's over: I can't bear to be in the same room as that person—I can't stand the sight of them.'

Hormonal changes can sometimes lead people to feel so strongly compelled to leave a relationship—even when that course of action may seem irresponsible or unjustifiable to others—it would be hard to criticise them on moral grounds. Some women, for instance, have reported that during meno-pause they experienced violent mood swings that included feelings of aversion to a partner they had loved for years. Not only do they seem powerless to control these moods, but they experience them as completely authentic: 'It's how I really feel—it's just that I was never prepared to say it before.' Later, they may feel bewildered by their own behaviour and quite unable to explain their determination to leave the relationship. Some men, similarly, have reported feeling powerless to resist hormone-driven passion that has led them to abandon a long-term relationship in favour of sexual excitement with a new partner. Again, such behaviour sometimes seems bewildering, in retrospect, to the men themselves, and they may simply say, 'I felt as if I had no choice.'

In other cases, people experience bouts of clinical depression, intense jealousy, panic, or other uncontrollable feelings that cloud their judgment about a relationship and cause them to believe, with utter conviction, that they must leave. In many such cases, the question of whether a partner was 'right' to leave is complicated by their sense that there was no choice—and if there really was no choice, then it ceases to be a moral question, even though the behaviour may strike many other people, including the abandoned partner, as 'wrong'.

Such cases may test the depth of a partner's love and patience, but they should not necessarily be regarded as raising ethical issues—except, perhaps, for a counsellor or medical practitioner who has given inappropriate advice or inadequate treatment. (In the same vein, a court may sometimes decide a crime was committed under conditions of 'diminished responsibility' and therefore treat the person who committed it more leniently than might otherwise have been the case.)

Decisions about the possible termination of a relationship are often complex, difficult and tentative. The issues are sensitive, the feelings of the people involved are delicate, and the likely consequences are hard to calculate. Such decisions appear fraught with additional moral implications when children are involved, when one of the partners wants to go and the other wants them to stay, or when one partner is racked by guilt about having fallen in love with someone else and is trying to come to terms with the possibility of losing either an existing partner or a new lover, or both.

The possible permutations and combinations are endless, but the core question is always the same: *Should I stay or should I go?* Once the question has been put like that, we are in moral territory. We have admitted that there is no easy answer, that there are ethical issues involved, that our actions will have an impact on the wellbeing of others and that we may be torn between the appeal of two or more of the 'ideals' to which we aspire.

For instance, we may believe wholeheartedly in the virtue of long-term, committed relationships, yet feel convinced that our children would be better off *not* living with two warring parents who don't love each other—or don't love each other *enough*. Or we may have explicitly committed ourselves to the ideal of loving someone 'forever' and 'unconditionally' yet feel that we ourselves are no longer being loved in that secure way. We may feel that staying with this partner is inhibiting our personal development and holding us—and them—back from seeking a new and more positive direction in life.

We may feel 'out of tune' with our partner, finding that as we have grown older we have each developed new interests or new friends that are not shared; each of us seems happier in circumstances that exclude the other. 'I'm passionate about writing poetry, but he just mocks me for it.' 'She is unsympathetic to my religious faith, and that has become increasingly important to me.' 'I'm fascinated by the share market, but he can't stand it and seems determined to act more and more like the hippie he always wanted to be.'

It might be a question of someone new coming onto the scene. 'He makes me feel alive in a way I've never experienced before.' 'She understands the real me—I've never felt as valued as I do when I'm with her.' Such sentiments are common enough, and it's easy to dismiss them as expressions of unbridled lust or inappropriate romanticism when you're watching from outside the relationship. But to the people who are in the grip of such powerful emotions, the moral issues are inevitably blurred by the intensity of the feelings involved.

There are no easy answers, and there are certainly no universally applicable answers. At such critical times in our lives, the need for moral mindfulness is acute: we need to weigh all the issues, all the factors, all the consequences, and then try to decide what's right for us, in this situation, taking all those factors into account. The process of visualisation can be helpful in clarifying our thinking. Imagine—*fully* imagine—staying in your present relationship, and then imagine—*fully* imagine—leaving. Immerse yourself in every aspect of both scenarios; then and only then will you be in a position to decide whether to stay or go, whether to openly discuss the issues with the partner you are contemplating leaving, whether to seek the help of an impartial counsellor, or whether to leave things as they are and let more time pass.

A woman who leaves her partner in order to 'find herself' may ultimately decide that self-discovery is a never-ending process (some people call it 'life'); on reflection, she might wonder if it would have been better to take things more gently, absorbing the stresses inherent in any intimate relationship, while ensuring she made some regular 'me time'.

But who knows? Having left the relationship, she may well find the sense of liberation, peace and fulfilment she was seeking, or she might be desolated by loneliness and distracted from her quest for self-discovery by the challenges of living without a partner. On the other hand, if she had stayed she might never have been able to break free from the sense of duty she found so oppressive. Either way, she may experience some guilt, some regret, some wistfulness, some lingering sense of 'what if?'

Outcomes are never certain, but careful visualisation, in a spirit of moral mindfulness, can minimise the risk that we will behave in ways that increase the suffering and diminish the wellbeing of all concerned—including ourselves. Often, the process of visualisation can actually be shared with a partner: in mature relationships, partners would usually prefer to know exactly what is at stake when the relationship is obviously in crisis.

A young man who has being living with his girlfriend for two years, and is on the point of agreeing to a formal engagement, finds himself attracted to a woman who works in his office and who symbolises a sense of freedom and excitement his present relationship seems to have lost. The more he sees of the other woman, the more stifled and uncertain he feels. He doesn't know what he *ought* to do, and he's not even sure what he *wants* to do. At times, moving out looks like the 'cleanest' solution, offering a means of escape from his dilemma and creating the freedom to explore the possibility of a more serious relationship with the other woman. Yet he also feels a strong moral obligation to his present girlfriend, he still loves her (though possibly with less intensity than previously), and their plans for some overseas travel are well advanced.

What should he do? Tell his girlfriend that he needs some 'space', that he wants to put their relationship 'on hold'? Or declare that 'it's over' and walk away (in the direction of the other woman, presumably)? Or should he spend some time with the other woman in the hope that his heart will instruct him that one of them is 'right' for him?

Does he really believe his previous enthusiastic commitment to his girlfriend was premature, or is he experiencing the natural hesitation of a young person who is about to start behaving like a stereotypical 'older' person—settled, stable, responsible, respectable? Has his existing relationship reached its natural end, or has it merely reached a point where it is challenging him to take more responsibility for the quality of the relationship and to rely less on the giddy momentum of romance?

If he goes, he may experience a welcome surge of liberation. He may pursue the 'other woman', only to find that she is as interested in *non*-commitment as he thought he was, but that, on reflection, he wants a more settled, reliable, exclusive relationship than she does. He may be consumed by an incongruous combination of jealousy and relief at the discovery that his previous girlfriend has quickly found someone else, and seems intent on marrying this new man. He may date a series of women, none of whom seem as much fun to be with or as close to being a 'best friend' as the woman he has ditched. He might yearn to return to the earlier relationship but with the boundaries more clearly drawn. Or . . . who knows?

His real challenge is to recognise the sound of the moral bells ringing in his head. This is not just a simple case of one romance running out of steam, so—*quick!*—let's find another. Here, a young man torn by doubt has raised the 'should' question in his own mind—a clear sign that he suspects there are moral issues at stake. That doesn't mean he *should* stay, but it does mean he should establish what the issues are, and then face them honestly.

Is he having a problem with the very idea of commitment? Has he failed to be frank with his girlfriend about the kind of relationship he really wants? Is he unsure of his love for her, or unsure of his capacity to sustain *any* relationship, year after year? Is he clear about what he wants and about how much he is prepared to give? Has he allowed himself to drift into something that looks like commitment, when it's actually more like inertia? Has his desire for easily accessible sex been posing as devotion? Would going cause more pleasure than pain for all concerned, or more pain than pleasure? Which ideals—which virtues—should he look to in his desire to make the 'right' decision?

Time for some moral mindfulness. Time for some visualisation. Time to immerse himself in the *going* and the *staying* scenarios, and to imagine himself, in a year or two, as the central character in both stories. The discipline of visualising two different outcomes will clarify his thinking not only about his feelings towards his girlfriend, but also towards commitment, romance and sex—and possibly even towards marriage, parenthood and a career as well. Thinking himself into the next step, and the next, will reveal something about his own motives, his own values—the things he can authentically bring to a relationship, and the things he can realistically hope to get from a relationship.

Whether he decides to stay or to go may not turn out to be the main point; the process of working through those two stories will teach him some important lessons about himself. If he stays, he'll be a stronger, more committed partner; if he goes, he'll know precisely how to explain his decision to his girlfriend, and how to handle his next relationship with more confidence, more integrity and more transparency.

Breaking up is never easy, but it might be no harder than staying, once the issues are out in the open. What's *really* hard is trying to make decisions that affect the well-being of other people without taking the necessary time for proper moral reflection.

13

Is tolerance an over-rated virtue?

The human race doesn't have a good record when it comes to our tolerance of differences—whether ethnic, religious, generational, gender-based or cultural. Wars have been fought over religious differences; families have been fractured by political and other differences of opinion; marriages have collapsed under the weight of one partner's intolerance of the other's musical or travel preferences, or even over their manners and speech ('How can I be expected to live with a man who holds his knife like a pencil and refuses to change?'). History is littered with stories of fiery racial intolerance, especially where it involves immigration. In the early nineteenth century, for instance, French workers rioted in protest against immigrant workers from England and Germany; in the late twentieth century, Fiji was rocked by an armed coup staged against a government judged to be too tolerant of ethnic diversity.

Yet most of us would like to think of ourselves as tolerant, because we regard tolerance as a virtue and we often feel ashamed of the passions that drive our prejudices against people with different religious beliefs, different political agendas, or, most particularly, different ethnic and cultural backgrounds. Racism is almost universally condemned, even by people who find themselves in its grip and who find it necessary to preface a racially prejudiced remark with the disclaimer, 'I'm not a racist, but . . .' Indeed, in multicultural societies, tolerance is sometimes elevated to the status of a *cardinal* virtue, as if it is the one thing on which social harmony depends.

So when we find ourselves thinking or acting intolerantly, we may experience a particular kind of guilt arising from the sense that we are not being quite worthy of ourselves; that we are exposing the dark side of our natures; that we are giving in to a rather primitive, uncivilised urge; that there's a nobler side of us that should be allowed to prevail. In short, most of us think intolerance is wrong.

Ironically, those nineteenth-century French workers' riots took place in the context of a recently proclaimed declaration of the Rights of Man that articulated the notion of equality and, by implication, called on people to accept their moral responsibility towards each other, regardless of race, politics or religion. Even today, when people express vehement opposition to an immigration program, they will often couch their resistance in terms that suggest they have nothing against foreigners, *per se*, it's just that they don't want them 'coming here and taking all the jobs'. In Australia in the 1990s, resistance to Asian immigration was often based on precisely those grounds (plus, for some Australian parents, an interesting variation on the theme: resentment of Asian children who 'work too hard and win all the school prizes').

Australians take some pride in their reputation for tolerance, especially their record of hospitality towards the huge wave of post-war immigrants who came here from southern Europe—though, as in most countries that have absorbed large numbers of immigrants, it actually took a couple of generations to embrace them fully: we loved their food before we learned to love them. But cracks regularly appear in this veneer of harmonious coexistence, particularly as new immigrants appear from countries that seem more 'alien' than those we are familiar with.

Diversity can breed intolerance

In July 2003, the Australian sociologist Dr Bob Birrell published some research that seemed to point to a widening gulf in Sydney between regions divided on both economic and ethnic grounds. In an article written for the *Sydney Morning Herald*, Birrell predicted the kind of trouble that usually springs from such divisions, and my own research at that time confirmed that racial prejudice in Sydney (and elsewhere across Australia) was on the rise.

Writing in the *Age* a year earlier, Professor Robert Manne had identified a wave of what he called 'Islamophobia'—the tendency of many Australians to draw the line at tolerance of the religious and cultural practices of Muslims and to express outrage at the number of Muslim immigrants being admitted to Australia. (In fact, by the time of the 2016 census, Muslims accounted for only 2.6 per cent of the Australian population.)

'Drawing the line' is hardly new for Australia. We once drew the line at anyone who wasn't white and only abandoned our 'white Australia' policy in the late 1960s. In *Claiming a Continent*, David Day describes the public outcry in 1936 when it was revealed that the number of residents coming from British stock had fallen below the accepted minimum of 98 per cent. (It had fallen to 97 per cent.)

After World War II, our attitudes to immigration underwent a radical shift, mainly because we urgently needed manpower to help us do all the work associated with the post-war economic boom in manufacturing, construction, housing and mining. Nevertheless, each new wave of immigrants has been met with some degree of resistance and intolerance from the host community: we wanted all those people to come here, but we also wanted them to 'know their place', to be suitably grateful, to be impressed by our culture, and not to impose too much of their own culture on us.

Towards the end of the twentieth century, we experienced a fresh challenge to our image of ourselves as a hospitable and tolerant society via a steady trickle of Vietnamese people seeking asylum, arriving in boats that seemed barely seaworthy. The term 'boat people' entered the language. Our initial resistance to the Vietnamese boat people soon mellowed into recognition that most of them were genuine refugees and that our humanitarian impulses should be responded to. Strong political leadership at the time exposed our intolerance and suspicion as sentiments unworthy of us.

Subsequent surges of intolerance in the early years of the twenty-first century were not inhibited by any similarly civilising influence. Indeed, by their own tough stance on refugees seeking political asylum in Australia and by condoning the harsh conditions in which they were imprisoned in detention centres, successive Australian governments appeared to be offering implicit encouragement to those who wanted to dehumanise refugees and to revile particular ethnic groups. (Iraqi and Afghan asylum-seekers were particularly out of favour, even though they had been fleeing the very regimes Australia had officially opposed.)

Such prejudices produce a kind of 'domino effect': when people feel they have permission to indulge one prejudice—against asylum-seekers, say—they are emboldened to extend their range, especially in a climate of fear induced by the threat of international terrorism and a continuing political emphasis on 'border protection'. So, in the early years of the new century, intolerance of 'illegals' seemed to trigger a fresh outbreak of *general* intolerance: Sydney's Lebanese community, for instance, suffered the ignominy of being stereotyped as 'criminals' in the wake of an ugly rape case involving a group of Lebanese men; Arabs were widely regarded with suspicion, as if, following the 2001 attack on New York's World Trade Centre, they should all be regarded as potential terrorists; Asians were being spat upon in city streets; and Indigenous Australians found themselves struggling to maintain previous levels of support and sympathy for their cause. In spite of Prime Minister Kevin Rudd's 2008 apology to the Stolen Generations, and supportive rhetoric from other politicians, the position of Indigenous Australians failed to improve. In 2017, the Aboriginal and Torres Strait Islanders' Constitutional Convention issued the so-called Uluru Statement calling for the establishment of a council of elders to advise the Australian parliament on matters affecting Indigenous people. That call was rejected out of hand by the then prime minister, Malcolm Turnbull, without parliamentary debate or community consultation. Indigenous leaders were understandably outraged by the government's unwillingness even to discuss the proposal with them.

Such expressions of prejudice and intolerance sit oddly with Australians' view of themselves; they represent a clash between the high-sounding values we claim to espouse and the moral indifference we claim to abhor. We therefore need to understand the social context in which this phenomenon has occurred. As suggested earlier, Australians have been suffering from a sense of growing unease, provoked by the destabilising effects of a series of social, cultural, economic and technological upheavals.

By the turn of the century, Australians were not only suffering from the well-documented phenomenon of 'reform fatigue' but also from its close companion: 'issues fatigue'. Globalisation, tax reform, the republic, foreign investment, population policy, youth unemployment . . . we had had enough. We wanted a break. We were ready to disengage from the national agenda, because it all felt too hard, too daunting and too far beyond our reach. So we retreated. We took our eyes off 'the big picture' and turned instead to the miniatures of our private lives and local communities. Feeling that 'issues' were beyond our control, we turned our attention to the things we felt we *could* control. We couldn't get enough TV programs about backyards and cookery; we couldn't get enough portrayals of cosy 'village life'; we couldn't get enough retail therapy.

The almost inevitable consequence of such a period of disengagement and withdrawal was that people became less compassionate in their attitudes towards the poor, the disadvantaged and others in need, less interested in political and social issues ('Leave us alone!'), and more protective of their homes, their children and their comfortable way of life—provided they were on the right side of the growing income-inequality gap. These are the very conditions under which prejudice and intolerance thrive, especially when combined with a vague sense of threat from international terrorism.

In such a climate, the question inevitably arises about whether 'we have gone too far' in welcoming various ethnic groups or even in tolerating the social changes wrought by the gender revolution. Hospitality and generosity give way to edginess and social exclusion. People who continue to stand up for the concept of multiculturalism and to advocate the virtues of cultural diversity and a progressive social agenda are accused of being 'bleeding hearts'.

Where should we draw the line?

Australia is by no means the most intolerant country on earth: indeed, our pride in our own levels of tolerance may be somewhat justified when we compare ourselves with many other parts of the world. It is humans, as a species, who find it hard to sustain social harmony in the face of ethnic and other forms of cultural diversity. Here is Theodore Zeldin in *An Intimate History of Humanity*:

> Tolerance is not the modern medicine it is made out to be, but an old folk remedy, with only short-term effects. Though some civilisations have enabled different races to live peaceably side by side, anger against foreigners and minorities has flared up again and again, often with a suddenness that catches them unawares. And even after centuries of experience, the tolerant are liable to be held in suspicion, or accused of lax morals.

In societies like Australia, the concept of multiculturalism has been widely embraced—though the word itself still makes many people feel uneasy. (Some prefer 'cosmopolitan' with its connotations of rich diversity.) But in any multi-cultural society, inevitable tensions arise from the process of

trying to synthesise different cultural myths, mores and practices—ethnic, religious and otherwise. So while we continue
to praise tolerance as a virtue, some doubts have emerged:
'The trouble is, we let other people walk all over us. We're
too tolerant. We bend over backwards to accommodate these
people, but would they do the same for us?'

Many people are troubled by such ruminations. On the
one hand, we accept that tolerance is morally attractive:
we should accept people as they are and acknowledge their
equality with us in a society that still clings to the ideal of
egalitarianism. On the other hand, should we be expected
to give anything up in order to absorb people from different
ethnic or religious backgrounds into our society? Should
Christmas plays no longer be performed in schools, for
instance, so as not to offend Muslim children and their families? Or should we be trying to incorporate all the religious
and ethnic flavours of the local community in a school's
cultural activities?

Clearly, tolerance can go too far if it encourages us to
suppress our own values, or to act in ways that are incon-
sistent with the dictates of our own consciences. We may
nevertheless find that we are prepared to modify some of our
attitudes and values in response to the experience of living in
a culturally diverse society: indeed, it would be remarkable
if that did not happen over time. But that is quite different
from feeling pressured to act in ways we actually disapprove
of, or tolerating behaviour by other people that impinges
directly on our personal and cultural freedom. There is no

virtue in the kind of tolerance that stands back and allows people to do anything they like, even when it is violent, illegal, destructive or offensive.

'Live and let live' is a good slogan for any society, but it becomes oppressive if we feel as if the pressure to 'let live' has been allowed to outweigh the freedom to 'live'.

Beyond tolerance . . . to understanding and acceptance

Even when a society experiences a wave of racial or religious intolerance, there's always an important caveat: people consistently distinguish between their negative attitudes towards generic groups such as 'ethnics' or 'Muslims' and their positive reactions to representatives of those groups who have become their neighbours, workmates or members of their social circle.

'My brother-in-law is a Muslim, and he's a lovely fellow,' said a respondent in one of my research projects, cutting across a diatribe against the negative influence of Muslims on Australian culture. 'There's an Iraqi woman at work who had an unbelievable time getting here. You can't help admiring her,' said another.

In our discussion of concepts like 'tolerance' and 'diversity', there is a risk of making diversity sound like an end in itself. In fact, diversity is only good for us if it's good for us; if it enriches our culture and brings sufficient benefits to offset the inherent, inevitable tensions.

Many people would claim that diversity does do those things, almost automatically; that it creates, by its very nature, an intrinsically healthier and more stimulating society than one that is more culturally homogeneous. Even in the world of work, there's a strong argument for saying that a deliberately diversified workforce can enrich a corporate culture and, in the process, make it easier for people from minority groups to feel welcome, whether as employees or customers.

Writing in the *Sydney Morning Herald* about workplace diversity, Rosanna McGlone-Healey quotes Paul Oliver, a one-time media adviser to the Australian Human Rights and Equal Opportunity Commission, who says that businesses benefit from diversity in a number of ways:

> Applying diversity principles means you choose the best possible people from the widest possible pool of potential employees. This draws on a greater breadth of skills, knowledge, experience and level of creativity and provides improved service to your diverse customer base. It increases productivity and innovation; diminishes conflict and grievance issues and enhances your corporate image as a responsible employer.

That sounds like a big call (and, from an ethical point of view, it would be better to set aside such considerations as 'enhancing your corporate image'). But Paul Oliver's claims closely match those made by Scott E. Page in *The Diversity Bonus* and by advocates of cultural diversity in society at large.

Yes, there's initially a painful period of resentment, suspicion, mistrust and adjustment on both sides of the cultural fence, but the more *personal* contact we have with people who are culturally different from us, the more we will gradually come to understand and accept each other—perhaps, for some of us, because we know that's the right thing to do, but mainly because it's part of a natural process of social and cultural evolution. (Australia's high rate of inter-marriage between people from diverse birthplace-groups means that multiculturalism in the Australian context actually produces a high degree of cultural integration.)

In the end, the advocates and opponents of a deliberate policy of 'cultural diversity' want the same thing: a rich and harmonious society. Some generosity of spirit is required to achieve that, and we occasionally need to remind ourselves that we are only striving for diversity *because* we believe the benefits outweigh the difficulties.

But if the word 'diversity' can trigger prejudice among those who remain sceptical about its benefits, an over-emphasis on the word 'tolerance' can be equally dangerous. For a start, it sounds rather patronising—like a pat on the head, or a seal of approval that can be withdrawn at any time. How would you like to be 'tolerated'? Wouldn't you prefer to be understood and accepted?

The moral issue here is actually quite simple: a moment's reflection will tell us that it is morally unacceptable to make judgments about anyone based on prejudice. It is unfair to assume anything about any individual based on stereotypes of the group to which that individual belongs. If we are serious in our commitment to justice, fairness, equality and freedom, then our belief in those things cannot be qualified on the basis of another person's ethnicity, religious belief, cultural background or gender. Prejudice, in any form, represents a repudiation of those very values.

The trouble with prejudice is that it closes our minds to other people's views, to the insights that new information might bring, or even to the possibility of mind-changing experience. As the pioneering American psychologist Gordon W. Allport expressed it: 'Prejudgments become prejudices only if they are not reversible when exposed to new knowledge.'

Perhaps we need to redefine our cultural challenge. Rather than thinking of a multicultural society as a kind of ethnic accident we must somehow learn to live with, why not approach it as a national work of art—a brilliant, complex, creative process being brought to fruition by people of goodwill.

We don't need more *tolerance* of immigrants, 'ethnics', Muslims, Indigenous Australians, refugees and people seeking asylum or any other minority groups; what we need is more *curiosity*. We need to master the art of getting to know each other better.

14

Is lying always wrong?

We live in a culture of lying. In *The Book of Tells*, Peter Collett asserts that we lie, at some level, to about one-third of the people we meet every day, especially those we are trying to impress. Collett quotes the work of Robert Feldman at the University of Massachusetts, who found that 60 per cent of the people who took part in one of his studies lied at least once during a ten-minute meeting; most of them told two or three lies in that time. Collett argues that without lies, our social life would soon grind to a halt.

Of course there are lies and lies (my personal favourite is 'I never lie,' uttered with a perfectly straight face). We normally think of lies as being words that deliberately distort or conceal the truth, but what about the unspoken lies lurking in our tone of voice (warm when we feel cool; sympathetic when we couldn't care less), our facial expressions (smiling when we feel hostile, laughing to conceal our insecurity or embarrassment, frowning to convey mock-sincerity) or our posture and gestures (calculated to convey an interest we don't feel, or to avoid the gestures that are sometimes regarded as tell-tale signs of lying—like scratching your nose, covering your mouth or avoiding eye contact)? Sometimes body language unintentionally exposes a lie, but it can be as deceptive as any words.

Is there a difference between the lie that is seriously intended to deceive for the purpose of gaining some advantage, and the lie that doesn't feel like a lie—not really intended to deceive, but only to lubricate the machinery of polite society? We often lie out of courtesy or in an attempt to protect someone else's feelings and it's true that many of the lies we tell, even though they are deliberately told, seem harmless enough. They may involve us in not telling the truth, yet they scarcely seem to be *about* truth-telling, in the strict sense. They are more like little niceties.

'Thank you for a lovely evening,' we lie, when we can't wait to get away from an occasion that bored or embarrassed or irritated us. What should we say? 'Thank you for inviting me', and leave it at that? That might be more honest, but isn't there some pointlessness about the kind of honesty that offends for no good reason? Better, perhaps, to play by the rules of the social game and make a note to be 'busy' next time you're invited to that particular place.

Make a note to be 'busy' next time, even if you're not busy? Again, it's hard to see the harm done by offering an excuse not to accept an invitation, rather than giving inevitable offence by baldly stating that 'I don't want to come.'

(Take care not to offer two or more excuses, though, or your response will sound suspiciously like a lie!)

We say to our children: 'I'm not angry with you' when it's obvious to them we are almost apoplectic with rage. Or we say, when the phone rings, 'Tell them Daddy isn't here.' (Wouldn't it be better to say, 'Daddy can't come to the phone right now. Can he ring you back?')

'You look great,' a man says to his wife when, in fact, she's looking a bit haggard or care-worn, but he knows she has had a tough day and a simple compliment might lift her spirits. The lie is an act of love.

'I look like a covered wagon,' said a friend of mine to her husband as she donned a new coat. 'Yes, but you look like an *expensive* covered wagon,' he replied in an unsuccessful attempt to make his wife feel better about being overweight.

Not everyone thinks such lies are harmless. From the Buddha to Immanuel Kant, some philosophers have taken a hard line on lying, believing that 'little lies' too easily snowball into the real thing, or that *every* lie, no matter how harmless, is a deception that should be avoided because it contributes to a culture of untruthfulness. (My first novel, *Little Lies*, was partly about this phenomenon: the central character kept dispensing those apparently harmless little lies of self-promotion we are all prone to tell, until he began to believe the 'big lie' about his own importance.)

Buddha's advice was uncompromising: '[One should] never knowingly speak a lie, neither for the sake of his own advantage, nor for the sake of another person's advantage, nor for the sake of any advantage whatsoever.'

Kant was even tougher: 'Its cause may be mere levity or even good nature; indeed, even a really good end may be intended by lying. Yet to lie even for these reasons is through its mere form a crime of man against his own person and a baseness which must make a man contemptible in his own eyes.'

In taking such a position, Kant is certainly being faithful to the very letter of the proposition that 'the end doesn't justify the means'. Yet, in practice, we distinguish between many different categories of 'lie' and we appear to attach differing degrees of moral significance to them.

When is lying 'right'?

The moral problem arises when you try to pick the point at which 'little lies' or 'white lies' or apparently innocuous 'social' lies become something more serious; when the deception has a purpose—good or bad—that goes beyond merely keeping the machinery of polite society running smoothly.

Sometimes, we harness our deceptions in the service of truth. If a battered wife sought refuge and protection in your home, who would criticise you for lying about the woman's whereabouts if her violent husband came knocking at your door? Kant's objections notwithstanding, who would say that lying was not justified if you contrived a lie that allowed you to escape from the clutches of a madman who was intent on doing you harm for no apparent reason?

What about a police officer who has to break the news to a distraught mother that her teenage son has been killed in a car accident? Suppose the officer had actually arrived at the scene of the accident before her son died and found the boy trapped in the wreckage, screaming in pain and pleading to be rescued. As the officer held his mangled hand and waited helplessly for the rescue squad to arrive, the boy's eyes were wild with panic and his face was contorted with anguish. It was the toughest death the officer had ever had to witness.

Nothing can bring this woman's son back; nothing can ease the pain of her grief. But, out of the kindness of his heart, the police officer tells her that at least her son didn't suffer: he was killed instantly. It's a lie.

If she reflects on it months later, when the fog of grief has finally begun to lift, the bereaved mother might wonder how the officer could have known such a thing, since he couldn't have been present at the moment of impact. He might have assumed that no one could have survived such a horrific crash, but how could he know for sure that death had come instantaneously? In the unlikely event that she does find herself reflecting so rationally on this appalling event—or even if the truth subsequently emerges at a coronial inquest—the mother is likely to feel grateful for the little myth that made the shock almost bearable, and eased her pathway towards some cathartic discussion of it with her family and friends.

That's no social lubrication; that's a clear case of a police officer distorting and filtering the truth out of his deep sense of compassion and in the belief that the whole truth could scarcely have been borne by the distressed mother at that moment. No advantage was gained by the police officer: his own courage was equal to the task of telling it as it really happened, but his judgment led him to believe that dumping a totally honest version of events on the mother would utterly destroy her spirit. He did not intend that the mother should be disadvantaged; on the contrary, although her pain may not have been measurably eased, she had at least a crumb of comfort.

Was the police officer right or wrong (or both at once)? And, given the choice, would that mother have chosen to be lied to in that way? If she later learned the truth, would she be angry with the officer, or grateful to him for protecting her the way he did?

Doctors dealing with patients who are terminally ill face a similar dilemma: depending on the age, the emotional state and the family circumstances of each patient, they have to decide how frank they should be in explaining the diagnosis, and perhaps giving an estimate of the time left to the patient.

Some people would say that it's the patient's illness, the patient's body, the patient's life, so the patient is entitled to the fullest possible account of what is going on. Few doctors would dispute that (though they might have in the past, when god-doctors were more prevalent than they are today) but many would still say that, in practice, it's not that simple. Many patients cling to the perfectly reasonable proposition that as long as they are alive, they wish to regard themselves as living, not dying, so talk of death is irrelevant: they are going to live life to the fullest extent possible, for as long as possible. They would prefer not to know all the details of their condition, and certainly not have a time-frame put on it, feeling that would be rather like 'pointing the bone' at them. In any case, such estimates are sometimes quite misleading: a prognosis that includes a precise time-frame may itself turn out to be 'a lie', even though it was presented in a spirit of frankness and, clearly, no deception was intended.

Wise doctors might give their patients a choice: 'How much do you want to know? I can tell you absolutely everything I know about your condition, including a detailed prognosis, or I can just tell you the bits you need to know in order to understand what's wrong with you and why I am proposing this form of treatment.'

If the patient is given the freedom to make that choice, the doctor is relieved of any sense that withholding information amounted to deception. In the circumstances of their approaching death, telling the truth to someone who wants to hear it is morally impeccable; telling the truth to someone who does not want to hear it is an act of brutal insensitivity.

Nevertheless, it is possible that we are too squeamish on the subject of truth-telling in such circumstances. Family members will sometimes argue with a doctor over the degree of truth that should be told, ignoring the possibility that many people would prefer to experience their death fully and realistically, including the sadness and even anguish that might accompany their sense of imminent departure from this world. Isn't that as legitimate a part of the experience of dying as the serenity and peace that others might feel in the same situation?

In *The Road Less Travelled*, M. Scott Peck argues that 'the reason people lie is to avoid the pain of challenge and its consequences—lying is an attempt to circumvent legitimate suffering'.

Even when we are acting out of such unimpeachable motives as love and compassion, we need to be careful that we are not resorting to lies to protect *ourselves* from the distress of witnessing someone else's distress.

If we are not careful, our lies might have the effect of robbing another person of the right to experience 'the dark night of the soul'—at the point of death, or in sickness, or in other circumstances where sadness and distress might be the most appropriate emotions. Not to be given the opportunity to experience these emotions might be to miss out on a crucial part of the experience of being fully human. After all, sadness is as authentic an emotion as happiness: it's less fun, but it's no less human, no less real, no less rich in what it can teach us about ourselves and each other. (And, no, this is not some stoic argument in favour of making people suffer: physical pain should be relieved to the limit of a patient's desire for relief, but some people will want to choose the richness of a fully experienced death, just as they may choose to experience the richness of grief in bereavement or divorce, undiluted by either lies or drugs.)

What emerges from such reflections is, to my mind, the unavoidable conclusion that although truth-telling is a virtue, it is by no means the supreme virtue. Compassion, tenderness, respecting the vulnerability of another person, humility . . . all these aspects of virtuous behaviour might, in certain circumstances, loom larger than the obligation to tell the truth.

Accepting that lying can sometimes be justified by appealing to higher virtues is a very different thing from abdicating our *general* responsibility to tell the truth. Saying of truth that 'it's only a word' or asking, rhetorically, 'what is truth?' can act as smokescreens, concealing the fact that telling the truth *as we see it* is a virtuous act: only in exceptional circumstances should we depart from that ideal. When, in a state of moral mindfulness, we reflect on the intentions behind the lies we tell and the consequences that flow from them, we will soon learn to distinguish between those told in the service of some higher virtue, those that were careless, stupid or unnecessary, and those that were mischievous or malevolent.

The best lie detector

We're quick to feel a sense of moral outrage when we discover that serious lies are told to us. It's true that we can often see through them, and it's even true that we sometimes wish to be lied to, but whenever we discover that someone has intentionally chosen to lie to us, it comes as a shock. We will often feel angry or disappointed about being deceived;

we will almost always feel as if we've been deliberately put at a disadvantage.

Similarly, when it is *we* who are telling the lies, we would generally claim to be able to tell the difference between social lubrication, innocent or well-intentioned lies told out of compassion for the other, and *real* lies that we know are wrong.

How do we know? How do we tell the difference? The tests for detecting real lies—bad lies, harmful lies—are simpler than the tests for making many other moral judgments. As with any moral choices we make, a good test is whether we would be embarrassed or ashamed if the lie were exposed, but the acid test is whether it is our intention not merely to deceive but to gain an advantage by the deception.

There are lies of *self-aggrandisement*, designed to give us a false advantage by seeking to impress someone, or to disadvantage someone else by having them unfavourably compared to us. For example, people who lie on their résumés, or in job interviews, are disadvantaging other applicants for the position.

There are lies of *compensation* when we attempt to make ourselves seem strong when we are actually feeling weak and vulnerable, or when we try to create an impression of trustworthiness to mask the fact that we have already abused the other person's trust—by passing on some private information about them as gossip, for instance.

There are lies of *treachery*, where we encourage someone to take an action that will ultimately advantage us, without revealing our intentions to them: 'I can see it's not going to work out for you two—you'll only be unhappy. You're not really suited. Why don't you give him up?' (I've had my eye on him for months.) 'I don't really think you should go for that job—not with two little kids and a husband who works full-time. Why not wait for a while, or go for something part-time?' (I've already applied for that job myself.)

There are lies of *insincere agreement* where we too readily fall in with other people's opinions or attitudes in the hope of pleasing them. This form of lying commonly occurs in the courtship rituals of romance, business deals and job interviews. The disadvantage to the other person arises from their being given a false impression of your true attitudes or values—a prescription for trouble when the truth later emerges, the eager early agreements are exposed as false, and questions about your integrity are inevitably raised in the other person's mind.

There are lies of *incompleteness* where we tell no specific untruths, but refrain from telling the whole truth: 'I had a good time' (and I had it with someone I don't want to tell you about).

There are lies of *silence*, where we fail to tell someone something they are entitled to know. Lies of silence are common when a person already in a relationship falls in love with someone else and fails to tell their partner. Partners who are kept in the dark are disadvantaged by not being told of such a radical change in their circumstances and are thereby prevented from being equipped to deal with the change. Lies of silence also occur in commercial transactions where sellers give buyers less information about the purchase than is available—a hidden problem with a car or a house, for instance, or incomplete information about the financial health of a company for sale—so they are disadvantaged in the process of trying to decide whether to buy or not.

There are lies of *emotional concealment*, where we might tell the literal truth about something, but fail to reveal the intensity of our feelings about it, or where we try to conceal our true feelings—saying, for instance, that we're 'fine' when we're actually feeling depressed or angry or rejected, or that 'it doesn't matter' when it actually matters a great deal. Such lies can cause difficulties between close friends or sexual partners, because they seem to imply the desire to exclude the other person from a previously established intimacy. They can also cause inter-generational tension: a mother might complain that 'you haven't told me what really happened' and her teenage daughter might complain that 'you never say how you really feel—and that's even more dishonest'.

And then there are the classic lies of *outright denial* where we refuse to admit to something we have done, in order to protect our own skin.

There's really no scope for ambiguity or ambivalence in relation to any of those lies: on any assessment, they are wrong. Unless you've worked hard at anaesthetising your conscience, every one of those varieties of lying will diminish you and make you feel alienated from your authentic self. Telling a lie is saying, in effect, 'This is not really me—I am not being true to myself,' so it is hardly surprising that we feel bad when we tell 'bad' lies.

But the full, unexpurgated, unpalatable truth about 'bad' lies is that we are sometimes relieved, rather than disappointed in ourselves, when we seem to have got away with lying—at least in the short term. The unfaithful spouse who lies to avoid a showdown may be intensely relieved when his/her partner seems to accept the story (though there's a strong probability that the lie will have been spotted and the partner will have decided, for any number of reasons—not all of them charitable—to let the lie pass and act as if the truth had been told). People who lie to mask their own untrustworthiness may feel buoyed up by the sense that, for now, they have created an impression of themselves that is more positive than the truth.

Yet lying triggers a negative psychological response in us: every lie we tell makes it easier to lie next time, but each lie also produces a subtle shift in our value system. Lying erodes our integrity, and we can usually sense when that is happening.

Do we sometimes want to be lied to?

There are many circumstances in which it looks as if we actually prefer to be lied to, rather than be told the truth. We especially love the lies that make us feel better about ourselves—lies told by friends, lovers, workmates or real estate agents. A bit of ego-stroking is quite hard to come by, and who can resist it? (Okay, so it's not strictly true that I am the most wonderful man who ever walked the planet, but I wouldn't mind hearing it occasionally from my nearest and dearest, even if it isn't uttered with total conviction.)

Plenty of people would rather not know about their partners' indiscretions because the prospect of breaking up a family seems worse to them than living with someone who might either be in love with someone else, or given to indulging in occasional romantic adventures. How often have we heard such people say, 'I don't want to know'?

Parents sometimes say the same thing in response to hints about the poor behaviour of their offspring—'I don't want to know'—and there's no reason to assume they are lying.

In the commercial marketplace, consumers sometimes want to be lied to: they want to have their tastes and preferences reinforced rather than challenged, even if those tastes and preferences could be shown to be irrational and unjustifiably extravagant. Many buyers of expensive cosmetics, for instance, don't want to be told that the ingredients are virtually identical to those in products that cost a fraction of the price: part of what they are paying for is the hope of a cosmetic miracle, and the prospect of that happening seems to increase with the price. (From a commercial point of view, then, is it wrong to put a hefty price-tag on hope? Or is it harmless? Does it add to the therapeutic effect of such a purchase?) Luxury car buyers, similarly, don't usually wish to know the truth about the real (and possibly quite marginal) differences between the expensive model they have bought and cheaper alternatives. (There are no more avid readers of luxury car advertisements than those who have recently bought the model in the ad.)

Readers of 'trash' magazines or tabloid newspapers don't always expect to be told the literal truth when they read salacious items of gossip about some celebrity or other. Part of the enjoyment of curling up with a magazine and a cup of coffee is the knowledge that it's all a bit of a game, and not to be taken too seriously. ('Anyway, how could they know exactly what Meghan said to Harry?')

In politics, the situation is a little more complicated. We claim to demand honesty and integrity from our politicians, though we are frequently disappointed. But there are occasions when it looks as if we actually *want* to be lied to (and politicians who sense this are no doubt happy to oblige).

Glen Newey, a political scientist at the University of Strathclyde, has concluded from his research that lying is an important part of politics in the modern democracy, and that, paradoxically, 'politicians need to be more honest about lying'. Newey believes political lying is partly a function of the greater exposure of modern politicians to media scrutiny (if only they were asked fewer questions, politicians would tell fewer lies!) and partly due to his belief that voters have 'the right to be lied to' in cases where they do not expect or want to be told the whole truth, such as during a war or national crisis of some other kind.

In 2001, the voters of Australia had a fair idea that senior Federal Government ministers were lying to them about the infamous 'children overboard' affair (when asylum-seekers attempting to enter Australia by boat were wrongly accused of having thrown their children into the ocean in an attempt to intimidate navy personnel into rescuing them and bringing them onto Australian soil), yet they voted that government back into office. There was evidence at the time of voters 'wanting to be lied to': many people remarked that even if the asylum-seekers had not thrown their children into the sea, 'they are the kind of people who would do that kind of thing'. In other words, some voters were more interested in having their prejudices confirmed than in getting to the truth of the matter.

On the eve of the 2004 Federal election, the 'children-overboard' affair was again raised when several former public servants and defence personnel questioned the veracity of Prime Minister John Howard's account of what he knew about the matter back in 2001. The Opposition sought to make this an issue in the 2004 election campaign by using it as a prime example of the alleged lack of integrity of the Howard government. And the voters' reactions? Many were simply wearied by the attempt to revive an issue that was three years old; others accepted that they had been lied to and went on to assert that this was of no particular significance to them, since 'all politicians lie'.

If Peter Collett is right, many lies are actually quite transparent to those on the receiving end: we are adept at picking up verbal and non-verbal signals that tell us whether we're hearing the whole truth or not. But that doesn't always mean that lies will be rejected outright: we weigh up the lie, the liar and the whole situation, and then we appear to decide whether we'll go along for the ride or not. In a surprising number of cases, we choose to go.

The most damaging lies are those we tell ourselves

We're good at railing against the political spin doctors or the advertising hucksters or the salesmen who try to sell us pre-loved cars that were only ever driven to church by little old ladies (though that's another lie we might quite like to be told). We're outraged when we find a shop has short-changed us, a product has been deceptively packaged, or an advertisement has misled us: 'That motel was nothing like the way it looked on the website. It was a dump and we paid a fortune for it—worst holiday of our life, *and* they have the hide to keep sending us little "come back soon" emails.'

We're disappointed in friends who don't level with us, or children who dissemble. We're furious with partners who lie to us—about where they've been, who they were with, or why they did something they knew would disturb, worry or annoy us.

We feel ashamed of ourselves when we know we have deceived someone else.

But the lies that really eat us up are the ones we are least likely to recognise: the lies we tell ourselves. André Comte-Sponville puts it like this:

It is sometimes legitimate, even from a moral standpoint, to lie to another person rather than tell him the truth. But one cannot legitimately lie to oneself, for to do so is to value oneself more than the truth.

Yet we do it. The British psychiatrist R.D. Laing (1927–89) observed that 'human beings seem to have an almost unlimited capacity to deceive themselves, and to deceive themselves into taking their own lies for truth'.

How do we lie to ourselves? We do it whenever we convince ourselves that a mischievous or malevolent lie was justified. We do it whenever we lull ourselves into thinking that a deception has been 'successful'. We do it whenever we fall for our own propaganda—whenever we allow those 'little lies' of self-promotion to grow, unchecked, into a grandiose myth about ourselves. We do it whenever we take ourselves so seriously that we rate our own importance and well-being above the importance or well-being of others. We do it whenever we assume that our own views should automatically prevail over the conscientiously held views of other people of goodwill. We do it whenever we decide that if other people want to treat us like a saint, a guru, a celebrity, or a superior being of any kind . . . well, why not?

(I liked this footnote to an article by my favourite Sydney sportswriter, Peter FitzSimons: 'David Campese and Peter FitzSimons between them played 108 Tests for the Wallabies. Peter Fitz contributed to seven of them.' I rather think Fitz doesn't lie to himself.)

To lie to myself is to erode my integrity and put my very sense of identity at stake. Who am I, this person who won't face the truth about myself; this person who prefers to live a lie, even in front of my own bathroom mirror, rather than accept who I really am, with all my frailties, shortcomings and flaws? Who am I, this person wallowing in self-satisfaction and self-centredness (or even, when the going gets tough, self-pity); this person who lacks the humility required to laugh at myself, the capacity to remain sceptical even about my own pursuit of virtue, and the ability to see myself for who I really am—human, mortal, and a mere speck in space?

Alienation from those we love is painful; alienation from ourselves is potentially lethal to the integrity of the psyche. If I haven't yet faced the truth about who I really am; if I haven't yet recognised the ways in which I try to deceive myself about my own motives; if I haven't yet learned to tell the difference between what I desire to become and what I have so far become, then I am not yet an authentic person.

But if I can accept and even learn to love the contradictory, complex and sometimes embarrassing truth about myself, I will be better equipped to recognise and tell other truths as well.

15

Business ethics or
[business] [ethics]?

Let's get one thing out of the way before we go any further. This chapter will not be proposing that 'good ethics is good business'. That's the kind of proposition put about in the aftermath of the 1980s—the 'greed is good' decade that brought so many business entrepreneurs undone. 'Okay, then,' the reasoning went, 'it looks as though ruthless self-interest won't always work, so—let's see—how about ethics? Hey, good one!'

Groucho Marx beat them to it: 'The secret of success in business,' he once explained, 'is honesty and fair dealing. If you can fake that, you've got it made.'

Ethics is not a business tool. We behave ethically in business for the same reasons we behave ethically in any other aspect of our lives: because we believe in the idea of doing the right thing rather than the wrong thing; because we aspire to live in harmony with certain virtues we hold to be important and worthy of our respect; because we know that a community—including a commercial community—cannot function fairly and justly unless we are prepared to respect each other's rights, needs and well-being.

It might happen to be true—indeed, many successful business leaders claim it *is* true—that when you conduct your business affairs on ethical lines, you will be more successful than when you don't. But such a claim gets us right back into the argument about rewards and punishments: if we behave with moral rectitude because we hope to gain a reward from doing so, we have missed the whole point of morality. (In case you'd momentarily forgotten, the only valid reason for doing the right thing is that it *is* the right thing.)

So we should regard the claim that 'in my experience, good ethics is good business' as nothing more than a statement of occasional happy coincidence. There's too much evidence to the contrary for us to make such a pragmatic claim the basis for a moral life—in business or out of it. Plenty of rogues and bullies prosper; plenty of cowards survive; plenty of people behave unethically without breaking the law and remain unscathed, at least in a commercial sense (we can't be sure about the state of their souls).

And, it must be said, plenty of people seem to succeed by following Groucho's advice—cultivating the style of a trustworthy and ethical person. Persuasive charm, sometimes carried to the point of mock self-effacement, is the stock-in-trade of those who engage in ethically dubious business practices: cutting moral corners; keeping one party to a deal less well-informed than another; engaging in activities that involve flagrant conflicts of interest; exploiting employees or customers; intimidating suppliers. Wheelers and dealers are often personally pleasant people—kind to their spouses and children, generous in their donations to charity, socially warm and amusing, smooth and expansive in their personal manner. But they can turn ugly, aggressive, arrogant and abrasive when it suits their purposes. It is the charm—sometimes suave, sometimes roguish—that allows them to get away with their unethical behaviour. ('I trust him; he's such a nice bloke—charming and generous; he wouldn't get up to anything devious.')

Are the moral rules different at work?

Properly understood, ethical behaviour can never involve the *exploitation* of other people for our own benefit: business is about satisfying customers' needs, not exploiting them. It's also about providing gainful employment for people and not exploiting them, either. Yet business activity is often characterised as being so ruthless, so competitive, so driven by single-minded self-interest that it does indeed end up creating situations where the strong can and do exploit the weak. That perception explains why so many people curl a cynical lip, or raise a sceptical eyebrow, when 'business' and 'ethics' are mentioned in the same sentence.

It's easy to imagine how the moral framework for business decisions could clash with a personal moral framework.

If that clash distresses us, we might do well to apply the 'death-bed' test described earlier: 'When I'm on my death-bed, will I feel better about my life if I know I ignored a moral imperative in favour of increased profit, or if I know I sacrificed a little profit in order to respond to a moral imperative?'

There have been some dramatic examples of companies unhesitatingly putting their profits at risk by the prompt recall of products in response to threats of extortion; many car-makers have enhanced their reputations by being prepared to admit and correct faults in their products as soon as they have been detected.

Since the primary purpose of business is to make a profit, the temptations to behave unethically are legion and the pressures of a competitive marketplace can encourage recklessness:

- You can improve the bottom line by exploiting the loyalty of your employees, expecting them to work longer hours than they are being paid to work.
- You can reduce the quality or quantity of your product without reducing the price.
- You can charge such a high price for your product that you are effectively exploiting your customers (though a bit of healthy competition might catch you out).
- You can collude with your competitors implicitly, by charging prices that unreasonably inflate the profits of everyone in the market, even if the collusion is not

sufficiently explicit to offend against the *Competition and Consumer Act 2010*.

- You can maximise the difference between the price you pay your suppliers and the price you charge your customers by under-rewarding your suppliers to the point of unfairness. Many small producers and manufacturers complain that they have been shamelessly exploited in this way by large retailers and powerful marketing companies—current examples of such allegations include the Australian dairy industry and the international coffee industry.

- You can develop marketing strategies that are intended to promote an unrealistic reliance on materialism as a pathway to happiness, or to mislead your customers into thinking a particular product or service will do more for them than it can actually deliver.

- You can abuse the implied trust that the community places in you when it allows you to market directly to children—for example, by creating advertising designed to raise their hopes unrealistically; exploiting their vulnerability by running competitions that 'soften them up' for the gambling industry; stimulating their greed in ways that might cut across their parents' attempts to teach them restraint; promoting unhealthy food and drink products in ways that appear both to permit and to encourage excessive or habitual consumption (especially bearing in mind the evidence that we are raising a generation of obese children).

- You can arrange your remuneration so you are personally rewarded to an extent that undervalues the contribution made by your employees or colleagues.
- You can promote your product misleadingly (though not necessarily illegally) by claiming 'beef' as an ingredient, for example, without mentioning that the meat in question may include parts of an animal that consumers would normally baulk at eating; you can claim performance characteristics for a car that are irrelevant to its legal use by drivers on a public road; you can identify your product as '97 per cent fat free' instead of 'three per cent fat'; you can mount a vigorous public relations campaign that suggests we should all drink more water than can be justified on medical or scientific grounds, purely to increase sales of bottled water.

We must assume that most business people would never dream of doing such things. Many, no doubt, do carry their personal values into their working lives and conduct their businesses with the same degree of integrity they bring to their non-commercial relationships. But many people, in and out of the business world, believe that business activity, by its very nature, throws up situations in which managers and employees either choose or feel obliged to violate their personal codes, partly because of economic imperatives and partly because of the culture of the organisations they work for. The 2018 banking royal commission revealed just how wide that gap between personal and commercial values can be.

On a large scale, people sometimes feel obliged to make far-reaching decisions about such things as staff retrenchments or plant closures or corporate takeovers and mergers, which may well be different from the decisions they would make if they were free to act purely in accordance with their own consciences. Even taking economic considerations into account, some people say that if it were left to their personal judgment, they would settle for less profit in order to maintain employment for people who have given the organisation loyal service over many years, but they believe that, in a public company, the tyranny of the share price precludes this possibility. Or they might believe, personally, that new technology should not be introduced because it will throw too many people out of work, yet feel that the commercial pressure to replace people with machines is inexorable.

On a much smaller scale, many employees report that they feel obliged to compromise their personal values 'to do things the way the boss wants', and that might range from the unsatisfactory or unfair way customer complaints are handled, to 'fiddling' the statistics in a performance report.

My own research has tapped into a feeling among employees that they are, indeed, expected to toe the corporate line, morally as well as commercially:

When you arrive at work, you leave your ethics at the door. It's like a coat you hang up before you go into the office. I have spoken up once or twice, but you get black looks. I even told the boss, and he just defended what was going on. So now I keep quiet and do what I'm told—I need the money.

It's like politicians—you might have high principles when you start, but you finally adapt to the situation you're in. If it comes down to a choice between compromising your principles or taking home your pay cheque, you'd have to go for the pay cheque.

I'm not at all happy with the way things are at work. I see lots of practices I regard as unethical. But the place is close to home and the hours suit me. Anyway, I wonder if it would be better anywhere else—I think maybe I'm not suited to the business world.

The dentist I work for talks to one patient about another all the time. He loves passing on all the juicy bits. Because he's so much older, I'm not in a position to tell him what he's doing is wrong. But I hate it.

Implicit agreement to cut moral corners in response to commercial or 'management' considerations can generate a moral climate within a workplace where people find it easier to behave dishonestly than they would in their private lives.

The 2018 Global Economic Crime and Fraud Survey conducted by accountancy firm PricewaterhouseCoopers (PwC) has shown a sharp rise in the number of businesses suffering from 'economic crime'—up from 36 per cent to

49 per cent in the past two years. PwC suggests the true figure may be significantly higher than that, since not all fraud is detected.

The most chilling figure in PwC's 2018 report is that 52 per cent of all corporate crime and fraud is perpetrated by people working within the organisation. As previously reported by PwC, most such crime involves employees 'ripping off' the company in some way—almost always involving the use of a computer—and the worst crimes involve payroll fraud. A partner in the firm had earlier referred to anecdotal evidence suggesting that people who commit corporate fraud are also more likely to lie on their CV.

The question is: are these people equally likely to behave criminally in their private lives, or is there something about the corporate culture they work in that encourages such behaviour?

The moral muteness of managers

'Did anyone stand back and ask themselves the simple question: Is this right?'

That was how Justice Neville Owen raised the fundamental moral issue in his report on the collapse of the Australian insurance giant HIH. The same question was implicit in much of the questioning of executives at the 2018 royal commission into misconduct in the banking industry. Reporting on the earlier HIH royal commission for the *Sydney Morning Herald*, Elisabeth Sexton described the examination of HIH's chief executive, Ray Williams, as revealing a man who seemed 'unable to find due north on his moral compass':

> No, it was not inappropriate that as chief executive he took board seats on organisations to which HIH made charitable donations of about $4 million a year. Nor could he appreciate why it mattered that when he was made a Member of the Order of Australia and received an honorary doctorate, the generosity to charities and research bodies identified in the citations had been 'overwhelmingly' provided by the company rather than Williams personally.

According to Justice Owen, such largesse was part of 'a consistent pattern of the group's resources being inappropriately applied for the personal benefit of senior executives, including executive directors'.

Questioning Rodney Adler, another director of HIH, Justice Owen sought a definition of conflict of interest.

'I suppose, speaking in a business sense, a conflict is when you do not have mutual interests, you are on the other side,' Adler replied.

'Or both sides?' asked the judge.

But, as Sexton reported, 'Adler could not grasp it.'

Adler was not alone in that. Many people have built their fortunes on the basis of activities others regard as morally dubious but, like Adler, they 'could not grasp it' or, perhaps, it has suited them not to grasp it, and to appear disingenuous in the face of criticism of such practices. Moral ignorance, insensitivity or paralysis (real or contrived) can make you a lot of money. It's like a moral version of 'emotional deafness'—the affliction that only allows us to hear what we want to hear.

We can easily imagine the kind of corporate climate that would discourage business executives—or politicians—from stopping to ask that simple question: 'Is this right?' And we can imagine how working in such a climate would gradually stifle moral debate until even those people who were acting in response to authentic moral impulses might feel embarrassed about saying so.

Thirty years ago, this problem of 'moral muteness' was identified in a landmark article in the *Californian Management Review* (Fall 1989) written by Frederick B. Bird and James A. Walters. They noted that managers seldom discuss ethical problems with their colleagues even though ethical issues frequently arise: 'Morality is a live topic for individual managers but it is close to a non-topic among groups of managers.'

Instead, Bird and Walters found, managers generally prefer to talk as if their actions were guided exclusively by organisational interests, practicality and economic good sense. Echoing the dangerous rubric that 'good ethics is good business,' many managers pass off their good treatment of colleagues, customers and suppliers as 'ways to succeed'.

Bird and Walters identified three reasons for moral muteness:

- The *threat to harmony* from raising issues which might reflect badly on other people in the organisation, especially superiors. Managers want to avoid appearing judgmental, especially when they are aware of the implicit deceits that pervade many organisations.

- The *threat to efficiency* in an organisation that might regard 'moral talk' as a waste of time. Managers often shun moral debate because they fear it may be interpreted as raising issues that are extraneous—or even antagonistic—to responsible management.

- The *threat to a person's image of power and effectiveness.* Ambitious managers want to appear powerful and effective: many of them apparently fear that moral talk would make them appear too idealistic.

The researchers noted that 'most managers neither know nor feel comfortable with the language and logic of moral philosophy'. The hazards in all this are obvious to anyone who hopes for a morally sensitive climate in business. Managers suffering from moral muteness will reinforce the idea—already abroad in many corporations—that management is an amoral activity and that economic considerations are paramount.

Bird and Walters concluded that 'it is impossible to foster greater moral responsibility by business people and organisations without also facilitating more open and direct conversations about these issues by managers'. Moral standards will have no compelling authority, they argue, until there is regular articulation of moral ideas and issues.

An employer's decision to sack someone, for instance, may appear to be a simple case of terminating someone's employment because they weren't doing a good enough job, or because the firm could no longer afford to employ them. But it's often also a moral minefield, peppered with awkward questions: 'Have I, as the manager, given this person enough opportunities to prove she can do the job? Is the fault really mine because of poor staff selection, inadequate training and supervision, and insensitive or incompetent management? Am I really sacking this person because I don't like her, or because I don't like the way she has shown up my own inadequacies? Are my reasons for firing her, however plausible they may sound, mere rationalisations? Will this sacking have a knock-on effect in which the person's self-respect will be so damaged as to affect other aspects of her life?'

Justice Owen pointed out that the starting point for the journey towards moral mindfulness at work is simple. We need only ask, regularly and audibly, *Is this right?* The evidence of the 2018 Banking Royal Commission suggests that this question is still not being asked often, or loudly, enough.

Has the 'invisible hand' disappeared?

Even among non-economists, the Scottish philosopher and economist Adam Smith (1723–90) is recognised as the father of the free market. Smith's book *The Wealth of Nations* is a seminal work in economic theory and the source-book for much of the zeal about free markets, right up to the present day. Smith is credited with having enshrined 'self-interest' as the currency of the market: he famously suggested that if the self-interest of buyers and sellers is given free rein, an 'invisible hand' will guide the operations of the market to the benefit of all concerned. Here are two key passages from Smith's classic:

> It is not from the benevolence of the butcher, the brewer, or the baker, that we expect our dinner, but from their regard for their own interest.

> [Within the free market] the individual intends only his own gain, and he is, in this, led by an invisible hand to promote an end which was no part of his intention.

The notions that benevolence has no place in commerce and that we would all be better off if markets were truly free (i.e. places where the untrammelled self-interest of buyers and sellers intersect) are the twin pillars of pure capitalism and so-called neoliberalism. But a great deal has changed in the world of commerce in the 250 years since Smith was writing and, in any case, those key ideas might be neither as brutal nor as simple as they may first appear.

Smith was a moral philosopher before he was an economist and his philosophical framework was presumably relevant to his economic theories. In *The Theory of Moral Sentiments,*

Smith wrote that 'there are evidently some principles in [man's] nature, which interest him in the fortune of others, and render their happiness necessary to him, though he derives nothing from it except the pleasure of seeing it.' One such principle is, according to Smith, 'pity or compassion, the emotion which we feel for the misery of others, when we either see it, or are made to conceive it in a very lively manner'. James Q. Wilson explores these propositions in *The Moral Sense,* and concludes that Smith's world-view was essentially benevolent. Wilson notes that, as a philosopher, Smith was particularly interested in the process whereby we acquire and develop a conscience.

So the famous 'invisible hand' of *The Wealth of Nations* may not be intended to convey the idea that, left to themselves, free markets will miraculously result in everyone being better off. It is more likely, given Smith's moral framework, that he believed markets would also be guided by the invisible hand of an inherently benevolent—or, at least, fair and trustworthy—attitude among all those participating in the market.

Some support for that interpretation came from John Harkness, former chairman of accounting firm KPMG, speaking at a 1995 conference on corporate ethics organised by The St James Ethics Centre in Sydney. Harkness bemoaned the loss of a sense of collegiality within professions like accounting and law, necessitating the introduction of more explicit rules and regulations. In Harkness's view, 'the battle is on' to maintain old-style professional standards that impose their own regulation on the behaviour of members of a profession, and always put the client's interests first. He spoke of the need to maintain a balance between strictly commercial considerations and the maintenance of professional standards, to ensure that the professions survive:

> If the profession ends, what replaces it? First, a free market, and then bedlam, an anarchy of accounting advice, a turmoil without standards, without ethics, without integrity . . . The professions must have the moral courage to maintain the balance against market pressures.

Twenty years later, Harkness's warning seems almost prescient.

In Adam Smith's day, markets were smaller and contact between buyers and sellers more personal. The handshake was a binding symbol of an agreement; a man's word was his bond. Trust was an inherent factor in the dynamics of the market in a way no longer possible since the advent of huge, especially international, corporations who need to rely on teams of lawyers to ensure the integrity of their transactions. To help their clients respond to the pressures of globalisation, the major accounting and law firms have themselves become part of this trend towards corporate giantism.

Smith's 'invisible hand' was not simply the inherent symmetry of market dynamics, ensuring the best possible outcome for buyers and sellers, but the equally inherent sense of *mutual obligation* between the individuals who operated in the market. Pride in the integrity of the market was a key factor in the operation of the invisible hand. Yes, it's true that Smith remarked that individuals intend only their own gain, but his reference to an outcome 'that is not part of this intention'—that is, the proper functioning of the market itself—suggests he expected there to be a spirit of goodwill on the part of all those apparently self-interested participants. In other words, he was assuming an inherent morality of the market based on the transparency of its transactions and the integrity of the relationships between buyers and sellers.

A key part of Smith's view of the free market was that all parties to a transaction would have equal access to information about the transactions in which they were engaged. Again, this was a symptom of the mutual trust on which an idealised free market would be based.

But today? Commercial confidentiality has become an obsession; manufacturers, distributors and retailers of products and services have access to far more information about the workings of the market than consumers do.

In the world of high finance, the contemporary style is to release only as much information as is legally necessary. In the present climate favouring improved 'disclosure' of information for the benefit of corporate regulators and share-market investors, some corporate boards take pride in finding ways to reveal the bare minimum, sometimes presenting even that in ways that are deliberately unclear. In the minds of some directors of public companies, concealment has become part of the art of disclosure.

Generous disclosure of information, fundamental to the operation of a truly 'free' market, has become deeply unfashionable and it is hard to escape the conclusion that this is part of a general retreat from moral transparency as well.

What should we make, therefore, of Smith's assertion that 'it is not from the benevolence of the butcher, or the brewer, or the baker, that we expect our dinner, but from their regard to their own interest'? Not so harsh, perhaps, when you examine it in the light of Smith's overall view of human nature. He is not saying that providers are *never* benevolent, nor is he suggesting they *should not be* benevolent, but simply that they have to make a living, so we can hardly expect them to give away their produce or sell it for less than a price that will return them a reasonable profit. The proper operation of the market, in other words, depends on sellers charging buyers a fair price; when they do, everybody wins (which is precisely what genuine free market advocates have always said).

In practice, many providers are both commercially astute *and* benevolent. Many butchers do their customers little favours, even today, and any organisation interested in winning and holding customers knows it must treat its customers like people, rather than impersonal numbers or walking bags of money. Making us feel better about ourselves—the goal of the enlightened marketeer—is a process that calls for a high degree of benevolence towards the customer. Successful marketing involves the creation of a good product or service designed to satisfy an identifiable consumer need, presenting it attractively and charging a fair price for it. Though the ultimate goal may be profit, the achievement of that goal will depend on a consistent attitude of benevolence towards the customer. The integrity of the marketing function demands nothing less.

Indeed, the modern mass-marketing ethic, unknown to Smith, is increasingly based on finding new ways of treating customers like friends, precisely because the marketplace has become so depersonalised. *Caveat emptor*—let the buyer beware—is no longer an appropriate slogan for any marketing organisation that values its customers.

This may be one reason why consumers seem rather less concerned about the impact of advertising on them than they used to be. My own research has revealed some softening in consumers' attitudes to advertising over time, partly because advertising is perceived as becoming more reflective of consumers' attitudes and values, and partly because the purpose of advertising is so transparent: 'It's not exactly rocket science, is it,' said a respondent in one of my surveys, 'they're simply trying to flog their brand.' In other words, advertising is seen as playing a game consumers also know how to play. (By contrast, news and current affairs programs are often seen as having a 'hidden agenda', perhaps driven by the bias of a reporter, or by the 'spin doctors' who control the flow of political propaganda.) In any case, consumers know what to do with advertising that insults, patronises or offends them: they ignore it.

In many product and service categories, successful brands have taken on something akin to a 'personality' that consumers use as a basis for making an assessment of the reliability, integrity, trustworthiness and even benevolence that Adam Smith expected of sellers in any truly 'free' market.

This is not to suggest that consumers now have an entirely benign attitude towards advertising; far from it. They may see it as easier to interpret—and perhaps reject—than some journalism and media commentary, but they are still alert to any attempt to manipulate them—or, even worse, to manipulate their children—and they still favour strict government controls over the content and quantity of advertising. Self-regulation of the advertising industry is regarded with scepticism among consumers who continue to believe that some advertisers will try to get away with whatever they can in their struggle for market share.

The disruptive advent of online advertising and the rapidly growing influence of IT giants like Facebook, Alphabet/ Google and Amazon will only serve to make consumers even more supportive of regulations that protect them from the insidious manipulation they fear from the new media technologies.

Consumers are also sceptical about the authenticity of competing brands that seem to offer few tangible differences between them. From the consumer's point of view, a 'legitimate' brand exists to expand the consumer's choice by offering a benefit not already available from other brands in the same category. When homogeneous brands begin proliferating in any market category, consumers are understandably inclined to question their integrity, to 'commodify' the category, and to rely more on price than brand reputation as a guide to the best buy.

Mass markets are, by their very nature, loaded in favour of the big, muscular marketing companies and retailers, which is why governments around the world continue to show a lively interest in consumer protection and to enact laws to regulate business activity. Zealots aside, virtually no one believes that, in the commercial and moral climate of the present, markets can be left entirely to themselves. The Australian Competition and Consumer Commission plays a central role in exposing unfair practices, and spotting signs of collusion, exploitation and manipulation of markets. Such interventions are presumably required because the 'invisible hand' of yore seems to have become invisible in a sense never intended by Adam Smith.

And in at least one other important respect, today's mass markets are different from those envisaged by Smith. In the intervening 250 years, and especially since the advent of mass production and international capitalism, the market has exerted its own influence on our psychology and our morality. In Smith's day, for instance, avarice was regarded as bad, compared with the virtues of restraint and moderation. Today, conditioned by the modern capitalist society's faith in economic growth, avarice and extravagance have become virtues, in the sense that they fuel the engine that drives the modern mass market.

The moral claims of stakeholders

Suppose you own a factory in a small town, where the community is heavily dependent on the jobs you provide—directly through employment and indirectly through the creation of demand for community services such as schools, banks, retail stores, doctors, dentists, vets, carpenters, electricians, plumbers, accountants, lawyers, government agencies and so on.

The factory's profits are in sharp decline because the market prefers cheaper products being imported by your competitors from China. It looks as if it would be sensible to close the factory and become an importer yourself.

Is this a decision for you to make alone, on purely economic grounds? Or is it a decision in which the workforce and indeed the whole town should be invited to participate? Who are the true 'stakeholders' in your business? What do your existing customers say about the products they are continuing to buy from you? Are there opportunities to refine your product, streamline your operations, produce a sub-specialty that commands a premium price over the imports, or make something else entirely? What are the views of your 'silent partners' in the business, who are only in it for the money?

Now suppose you are the chief executive of a major bank and your personal remuneration is tied to the bank's share price. You have a five-year contract and, the world of business being as it is, you have no grounds for believing your contract will necessarily be extended. On the other hand, the thing most likely to convince your board of directors to keep you on is—surprise, surprise!—a steady rise in the value of the shares in the company. So whether you are to stay or go, your personal financial future is heavily reliant on the performance of the bank's shares while you are at the helm.

Your predecessor closed dozens of branches, computerised many of the bank's operations and shed thousands of jobs. The bottom line was enhanced by all these measures and he walked away with a huge payout, reflecting the resultant lift in the share price. But customers are angry, staff morale is low and now the share price has plateaued again.

You would like to re-open some branches and enrich the quality of personal contact between the bank and its customers. You would like to trim fees, especially for less well-off customers (though the bank's current policy is only to trim fees for its wealthiest customers). You are concerned about the level of credit card debt being carried by many of your customers and you wonder whether the bank has some moral responsibility to encourage them to reduce that debt and become more prudent in their money management, though the bank's income may be somewhat diminished if that initiative were successful.

You believe that if more attention were paid to staff training and morale, and more time devoted to improving customers' experience of the bank, this would achieve long-term improvements in the bank's financial performance, partly through a higher rate of customer retention and a reduced need to be trying to win new customers all the time.

You are constantly being forced to keep an eye on the share price, day-to-day, week-to-week, and to acknowledge that some of the measures you want to take will involve a short-term sacrifice of profit as more staff will need to be employed to man the new branches and more time will have to be devoted to staff training in order to improve the quality of customer service. Among your senior colleagues, and on the board, there's a lot of talk about keeping the 'stakeholders' happy, but it usually comes down to *one* crucial stakeholder: the shareholder. Market research tells you that customers already believe the bank is more interested in its shareholders than its customers, and that this has implications for customers' perceptions of the ethics of the organisation.

As far as stakeholders are concerned, there are three broad groups: employees, who rely on the bank for their livelihood and, in many cases, for their sense of identity and self-worth; customers, who rely on the bank to meet their demand for financial services, efficiently and pleasantly delivered; and shareholders—especially institutional shareholders who are not remotely interested in levels of customer satisfaction or staff morale, per se, but only in the share price.

Customers and employees feel strong emotional connections with the bank; shareholders are there for the money. Employees do productive work and customers are the source of profits. Shareholders do no productive work at all, yet they carry the biggest stick. Is that fair? And what should we do about it? How might we hold those three groups of stakeholders in tension, based on their equal importance to the bank?

One of the things you might conclude from those two scenarios is that chief executives earn their salaries. But you might also recognise that tensions between moral and economic imperatives are difficult to resolve. Often, senior executives are required to make decisions that are morally unpalatable to them, but there remains the challenge of implementing even those decisions in the most morally sensitive way possible.

Consultation is usually the key: people who are going to be affected by a decision have the right to be consulted before that decision is made. If the decision is ultimately unfavourable to them, then, as employees or customers, they have a right to have the decision explained honestly to them and they will at least have the comfort of knowing their views had been taken into account. Customers can go elsewhere if they're unhappy; employees being retrenched, or disappointed in some other way, might find it harder to secure similar work elsewhere. They are morally entitled to be given whatever help can reasonably be provided— financial and psychological—in coming to terms with their sense of loss.

While the whole capitalist enterprise depends on investors being prepared to put money into corporations, moral issues surely arise when wages are held down, employees retrenched in large numbers, suppliers' margins squeezed, services withdrawn from communities dependent on them . . . all in the name of maximising short-term profits so as to improve returns to shareholders, whether as capital gains or dividends. Shareholders expect the best possible return on their investment, but are they entitled to that at the expense of other stakeholders?

Most state legislatures in the US have recognised the importance of other stakeholders by passing laws that give boards permission to resist shareholder pressure during mergers or takeovers. According to Marjorie Kelly, publisher of the US journal *Business Ethics* and author of *The Divine Right of Capital: Dethroning the Corporate Aristocracy*, 'these so-called "stakeholder statutes" allow directors leeway to *not* maximise shareholder gains. A board can legally refuse the highest offer for a company if doing so benefits other stakeholders, such as employees or the local community.'

Kelly argues that the dominance of shareholders' interest has become, in effect, a form of entitlement. For Kelly, 'entitlement has no place in a free market'.

But do we really have to wait for legislation to force us to recognise the moral claims of other stakeholders and to acknowledge that such claims will sometimes outweigh—or at least be equal to—those of shareholders?

Good work

In the early years of the twenty-first century, anecdotal evidence was emerging from both the corporate world and academia that suggested a new breed of young adults was entering the workforce—the leading edge of the Millennials—a generation who seemed more likely than their predecessors to be interested in the values of the organisations they were considering working for. Employers who could once talk to potential recruits—fresh university graduates, in particular—as though such people would be fortunate to get a job in the company or firm ('Are you good enough to work here?') now found themselves having to face a question being posed to *them* by potential employees: 'Is this an organisation worth working for?'

At its extreme, that trend was reflected in young people who would only contemplate 'altruistic' work—doing something they judged to be 'worthwhile'—rather than simply earning a living. It was also reflected in the sharp rise in the number of young entrepreneurs determined to do things their own way, according to their own values.

As the employment market has tightened, it is unclear whether that culture-shift has held. Some employers regard the demands of Post-Millennials now entering the workforce as being more typically self-centred than altruistic, but as community esteem for big business continues to erode, it is fair to assume that many potential employees will want to raise the question about an organisation's integrity.

No doubt most of us would like to think we are working for 'good' organisations, but for people at any stage of their working life, the real moral question is not only about where you work, but how conscientiously you take moral questions into account in whatever work you do. Moral mindfulness is as crucial at work as anywhere else. The moral climate of our workplaces is unlikely to improve until *Is it right?* becomes a stock question whenever business decisions—large or small, corporate or personal—are being made.

16

Should the state authorise the killing of its own citizens?

Apart from the possible use of lethal injections in both cases, legalised euthanasia and capital punishment might appear to have almost nothing in common. One is generally motivated by compassion and the other by revenge—representing opposite ends of the spectrum of human emotions—and yet they are linked by two significant moral questions:

- Is it ever appropriate for the state to intervene in the timing and manner of a person's death?
- What is a society saying about the value it places on human life when it decides to legalise the killing of any of its citizens?

From time to time, there's a surge of interest in both euthanasia and capital punishment—usually stimulated by stories in the media about a terminally ill person who is pleading for a controlled and dignified death, or a criminal who has committed such an appalling crime that the community is baying for blood.

Although the two issues tend to be raised by quite different groups of people with quite different agendas, the moral connection between them is inescapable. Yet they are rarely linked in public debate, perhaps because most people seem to be clear in their minds—one way or the other—about capital punishment, whereas the moral issues surrounding euthanasia seem more complex and attitudes are correspondingly more confused and tentative.

Capital punishment

Supporters of capital punishment argue that if a person is unambiguously guilty of a sufficiently horrendous crime, it is appropriate for society to exact commensurate retribution: 'an eye for an eye and a tooth for a tooth'. The argument is sometimes extended to say that taxpayers should not have to bear the cost of incarcerating ruthless and remorseless killers.

The tired old argument that capital punishment serves as a deterrent has long been discredited by the evidence. In Australia, for instance, there has been no perceptible rise in the murder rate since capital punishment was abolished: the last execution was in 1967, but the murder rate has been remarkably stable for a hundred years. In the US, states that impose the death penalty have roughly the same murder rates as those that don't. Why should we expect it to be otherwise? The passions that lead someone to commit murder—premeditated or unpremeditated—are unlikely to be stilled by considerations of the possible punishment. (It is presumably one of the characteristics of people who commit murder that they give insufficient rational thought to the consequences of their crime.)

Opponents of capital punishment generally mount four arguments against the use of the death penalty. First, you can't always be absolutely certain of the guilt of a convicted person, and history has produced some tragic examples of innocent people having been executed. Second, no one should ever be regarded as being beyond the possibility of redemption and rehabilitation: even one case in a hundred makes the attempt worthwhile. Third, no civilised society should legalise the killing of any of its citizens, no matter how appallingly they might have behaved, because that diminishes the value it places on human life. Fourth, capital punishment denies us the opportunity to forgive a person who has committed a serious crime, and the loss of that capacity diminishes us as a society.

The first argument can be refuted, since it is possible to imagine how the guilt of a particular criminal *could* be established beyond any doubt. The second argument is stronger but it is possible to imagine a case where a particular criminal seems so utterly remorseless as to be beyond the reach of redemption. But the third and fourth arguments have irresistible moral force because they can confidently be applied in all cases. Arguments based on the value we place on human life and on the civilising influence of forgiveness draw their strength from the fact that they cannot change from case to case: they are arguments about the values embedded in our culture.

If we believe that the state should execute some of its citizens, then the question of *which* citizens will always be open, at least theoretically. Today, we might agree that only criminals who meet certain criteria should be executed, but circumstances might arise in the future where we want to extend the criteria, perhaps under the influence of a wave of public hysteria about drug dealers, or child sexual abusers, or witches, or . . . who knows?

When there is no scope for legal execution, there is no scope for abuse of the principle that we should value every human life at least to the extent of preserving it, no matter how repugnant some people's behaviour may be to us. Similarly, by refusing *ever* to invoke the death penalty, we preserve at least the possibility of forgiveness.

Legalised euthanasia

There are seductive arguments on both sides of the euthanasia debate, but most of them are designed to appeal to our emotions through heart-rending accounts of particular cases. The challenge is to focus on the central issue: is it a good idea for the apparently widespread and well-motivated practice of euthanasia to be *legalised*? It is one thing to face moral choices about euthanasia, whether voluntary or involuntary; it is quite another to decide whether the state should be involved.

Let's first clarify what we're talking about. Euthanasia is generally defined as 'mercy killing', but that can take several different forms. Voluntary euthanasia can amount to assisted suicide—that is, responding to a request from a terminally ill patient to help them take their own life (for example, by supplying painkilling drugs which can be taken in a lethal dose). In cases where patients request some medical intervention to relieve their suffering and end their lives, euthanasia involves taking those active steps with the patient's knowledge and assent. But 'mercy killing' is perhaps most commonly understood as referring to cases where family and medical advisers decide, in the absence of any specific request from the patient, that terminating the patient's life would be compassionate, considerate and responsible. In that case, the decision may be based on the conviction that the patient should be terminally relieved of unbearable pain or indignity, or that the patient is effectively 'dead' anyway and no further medical intervention should be used to maintain such a poor quality of life (for instance, where the patient has been in a coma for some time and is only being kept alive by some form of artificial life-support system).

The fact that there are such diverse meanings of 'euthanasia', and so much uncertainty and disagreement about its moral status, highlights the need for moral mindfulness to help us make the right decision *for us* in our particular circumstances. We might even find ourselves reaching different conclusions on different occasions. Here's a friend's account of just such a difference:

> *When Geoff was obviously dying from cancer, he was in such pain that he pleaded to have all treatment stopped so he could go quickly. I was very unsure about it and I talked to the doctor who was looking after him in hospital about what would be involved. He said a 'breakthrough' dose of morphine would be required, and I knew what he meant. Before I could decide what to do, the palliative care people said they wanted to try a different approach to pain management and Geoff agreed to go along with that. Within a few days, he was feeling more cheerful and demanding that the doctors try everything possible—every kind of treatment—to keep him alive. He only lasted a few more weeks, but they were good weeks for him until the last few days, when nothing seemed to help.*
>
> *On the other hand, when my mother was so depressed and frail and pneumonia finally took hold of her, the doctors asked me if I wanted her to go on antibiotics and I said 'no'. I didn't even hesitate. She'd suffered enough already and I thought it was time to let her go in peace. So we agreed they would just try to make her comfortable with morphine. She was dead within twelve hours.*

Arguments in favour of euthanasia itself are not the same as arguments in favour of its legalisation (i.e. control by the state). What if both the situations described above had been subject to state control of euthanasia? Would that woman have felt as free to make the decisions she did, purely on the grounds of compassion, and even to change her mind in the first case?

Euthanasia is a fact of life: many terminally ill people secure the co-operation of their doctors and the support of their families in reaching the decision that, under certain circumstances, they would want to be relieved of their suffering through a humane and dignified medical intervention or through the withdrawal of an existing intervention. (Some, of course, take matters into their own hands.) In cases where a patient is no longer conscious, doctors do, in practice, sometimes advise family members that the withdrawal of life-support would be appropriate.

At present, none of these measures requires the bureaucratic intervention of the state: indeed, under our laws, provable cases of mercy-killing still theoretically count as murder, though we are taking an increasingly liberal and humane approach to the application of those laws.

So what are the arguments for and against legalised euthanasia?

Supporters of legalisation argue that because euthanasia is morally 'right' in certain situations, it should therefore be made legally 'right' in those situations as well. Everyone is entitled to a dignified death, they say; people in pain, distress or despair who want to die should therefore be supported in that wish without their family or doctors running the risk of prosecution. Supporters argue that no good is served by prolonging a life that has lost all apparent value and meaning to the person concerned and that, to prevent abuses of euthanasia, its practice should be controlled by legislation.

Opponents say the quality of palliative care is so good nowadays that no one need suffer a painful or distressing death; that a cure is always a possibility, however remote; that the reality of mercy-killing (by ever-increasing doses of morphine, for instance) is incidental to the process of pain control and should not be constrained or inhibited by a legalistic approach; that the creation of bureaucratic machinery to control euthanasia may well increase the chance of unwarranted terminations—for instance, on the initiative of impatient or uncaring relatives of a terminally ill person, or in cases where people are not terminally ill but have simply 'had enough' and want someone to facilitate their exit.

These arguments—pro and con—tend to blur at the edges of particular cases. What shall we say about Geoff, who wanted to die but who floated contentedly on a cloud of morphine-induced detachment for a while longer? If the legal machinery for the termination of his life had been put in motion, would that have increased pressure on his wife not to change her mind in response to the suggestion of a different palliative care regimen? And would the palliative care experts have bothered to come up with a new regimen, if they had known the legal process was already under way?

What shall we say about a person desperate to go yesterday, but unexpectedly sustained today by the sight of a new grandchild brought to the bedside? What about a person whose life has deteriorated to the point where it appears to be without value, but who, out of the blue, suddenly says something remarkable—some wisdom imparted, some comfort given to a loved one, some glimpse afforded of life-affirming courage or peace or pleasure that provides unexpected inspiration to relatives and friends: 'How grateful we were that we hadn't pulled the plug, when he came to, just for those few moments, and seemed so pleased to see us all. It was like saying goodbye.'

No question as serious as the *legalisation* of euthanasia should be settled by an appeal to examples like those. Although individuals will make their own moral choices, when it comes to legalisation a general principle must be found that transcends particular cases, but gives individuals freedom to exercise compassion and reduces (to zero, if possible) the chance of euthanasia being abused as a process.

As with capital punishment, one principle that could be applied universally is that human life should be valued to an extent which puts it beyond the control of the state. This wouldn't mean that we would no longer condone euthanasia: it would mean that, as now, we would leave it to the discretion of individuals—patients, doctors and families—to act with responsibility, sensitivity and discretion.

Yes, there would be abuses: pathological medical practitioners would still kill elderly patients under the guise of euthanasia, and some relatives would still be too quick to decide that the 'worthless' life of an elderly relative should be terminated. Such things no doubt happen occasionally now, and would continue to happen occasionally whether euthanasia were legalised or not.

Legalisation might actually increase those risks, by making euthanasia seem like an ever-present option—rather like an automatic extension of palliative care. In any case, what would it say about us, as a society, if we created a procedure for the systematic killing of people who met some bureaucratically determined criteria? Like capital punishment, once the decision to legalise had been made, the criteria—and the safeguards—would be exposed to possible modification.

Perhaps we don't need a law to say when or how euthanasia can happen; perhaps we only need the reassurance of knowing that loved ones who help the terminally ill to a dignified and painless death, in close collaboration with medical practitioners, could never be prosecuted for doing so.

Abortion

It may strike you as odd that a discussion of abortion is included in a chapter headed: 'Should the state ever kill its own citizens?' Even the most vigorous anti-abortionists would be hard pressed to find a definition of 'citizen' that included an unborn foetus. Yet there's some logic in considering abortion along with euthanasia and capital punishment, if only because so many people—especially those from the religious

Right—regard abortion as rather like killing a baby and therefore want to make it a legal issue, rather than a moral and medical one.

At its most extreme, the anti-abortion argument (often portrayed as 'pro-life') wants to equate the medical termination of a pregnancy with murder, and to have doctors who perform abortions treated as serial killers. Less extreme positions also depend on the assertion that the foetus is, in effect, a person who should be entitled to the same legal protection as any other person.

So that's the first issue: is an unborn foetus a 'person' in the same sense that a postnatal human being is? Straightaway, we can see one of the key difficulties in this debate: the problem of locating answers to questions about abortion on a continuum of possibilities.

A foetus that has almost reached maturity is *close* to becoming what we would normally recognise as a person, but a fertilised ovum isn't, though it is 'alive'. Between those two points lies a range of gradations that make black and white judgments difficult.

Any consideration of the moral issues surrounding abortion needs to acknowledge that spontaneous abortions are a natural part of the reproductive process. In fact, gynaecologists estimate that about 30 per cent of all pregnancies terminate in spontaneous miscarriage. About 80 per cent of those spontaneous abortions occur in the first thirteen weeks of pregnancy, half of them due to foetal chromosome abnormalities. Many women experiencing miscarriages very early in pregnancy are unaware of having been pregnant: they might assume they'd had a heavier than usual menstrual flow or an untimely period. Even if they half-suspected a miscarriage, such women would not be expected to react as they might to the death of a child.

When women are fully conscious of what has happened, they are still unlikely to grieve in the way they might be expected to if they had lost a newborn baby rather than a foetus. It's true that mid- and late-term miscarriages can be extremely distressing to the parents, but even though they may experience a deep sense of loss—the loss of the *idea* of a child—few parents who have experienced miscarriage would equate their loss to the death of a child. The difference is both obvious and significant; the earlier in a pregnancy it happens, the more obvious that difference will seem.

The philosopher Peter Singer defines a person as 'a rational and self-conscious being' and on this definition, an unborn foetus doesn't qualify. But if we stretch the definition to include the idea of a *potential* person, that changes the situation somewhat. When is the potential so close to *actual* that a foetus should be regarded as a person? On this point, there is so much disagreement among thoughtful people—including philosophers, doctors, biologists, theologians and lawyers—it is fair to suggest that this is a matter to be settled by each woman, preferably involving her sexual partner, after appropriate moral reflection on the issues involved and the likely consequences for all concerned.

In *Being Good*, Simon Blackburn, Professor of Philosophy at the University of Cambridge, has this to say about the concept of the foetus as a potential person:

> 'Potential' is a dangerous word ... An acorn is a potential oak-tree without itself being an oak-tree. My car is potential scrap, but it is not scrap, and its being potential scrap does not justify anybody in treating it as scrap.

Following Blackburn's line, we might also remark that a live person is a potential dead person, but that doesn't justify treating the live person as if it is already a corpse. Such analogies are somewhat specious, since there's no real argument about the difference between a live person and a corpse. But there *is* real argument about the difference between a foetus and a person, though many people would say the difference is self-evident—one is born and the other is unborn. The gradual, continuous nature of foetal development, almost imperceptible from one moment to the next, makes such a judgment seem a bit heartless and also a bit pointless: virtually no one believes aborting a foetus near full-term is a good idea unless there is a medical emergency that threatens the mother's life.

Some people therefore try to settle the question by choosing *the moment* when a foetus should be regarded as having the right to protection. They might insist that when the foetal heart starts beating, or when brain function can be detected, 'potential' has been established. Others suggest that the magic moment is when the mother feels the baby moving inside her.

Those who want to adopt a legalistic approach to abortion insist that the line must be drawn *somewhere*: four months, say, or three, or five. But if we are to see abortion as a moral issue, such precision will be unhelpful. The issue is not *when*; the issue is whether, under certain conditions, we accept that it is morally acceptable for a woman to procure the termination of a pregnancy.

Those 'certain conditions' will presumably include a medical opinion about the safety or otherwise of the procedure, given the stage reached by the foetus. Another factor to be taken into account will be the psychological and physical state of the mother and, perhaps, her domestic and financial situation. Where the partner is present and involved, their attitude will obviously need to be taken into account. Black and white assertions are unlikely to be helpful: if we merely state that 'a woman is in control of her own body', as if no other moral considerations arise, might we find ourselves having to support abortion in cases where we might otherwise feel some moral queasiness? What will we say of a woman who seeks an abortion because she feels that either an advanced state of pregnancy or the birth itself would come at a difficult time for her—clashing, perhaps, with the need to devote herself to the care of a terminally ill parent, or the deadline for her PhD thesis? She wants a baby, yes, but not *this* baby. In the future, biotechnology might offer such a woman radical alternatives to the removal and destruction of the foetus. She may one day be able to abort the foetus, store it, and resume the pregnancy at a more convenient time. Would that affect our perception of the moral issues involved?

While it is never our business to judge other people's moral choices, but only to encourage them to recognise the moral dimension of the choices they make, we might privately feel that such reasons for terminating a pregnancy appear highly debatable when compared with, say, a teenage girl who has been raped, a single mother of four whose pregnancy was the result of a fleeting moment of passion with a man she has not seen since, or a brain-damaged woman who sought love in the arms of a carer who now wants nothing to do with her. And what of a perfectly healthy, competent woman who does not want to be a mother, or who feels she has already produced enough children and whose contraceptive arrangements failed her? Or the woman who thought she wanted a child until she found herself pregnant, and then felt completely unable to go through with it?

It may not be appropriate for us to make any judgments about these women's choices (partly because we never really know what is going on in another person's mind, even when they claim to be telling us), but it *is* appropriate for us to encourage a state of moral mindfulness in anyone contemplating an abortion. As with all other moral choices we make, there may not be a general answer about whether or when an abortion is right or wrong, but there will be a right answer for each person in each situation. Contemplation will get you there.

And the role of the state? Given the complexity of the issue, it's hard to see how the state could justify taking control of the decision-making process away from pregnant women, their partners and their medical advisers. Equally, it's hard to see how the state could prevent women from obtaining an abortion once they have decided an abortion is right (or even necessary) for them. Women will always seek abortions, for all kinds of reasons, and if the procedure is both outlawed and aggressively policed, then a 'backyard' abortion industry will once again thrive, as it has in the past, with all the attendant problems of excessive fees, inadequate medical supervision and the creation of guilt and shame among people who, having made a responsible moral decision, should be respected for that.

17

Should we ever go to war?

Let's begin in the playground.

Everyone knows Terry and Jeff are bullies, and most of the boys in Year 7 have aligned themselves with one or the other. A few loners have stayed outside both gangs and formed a loose association of neutrals. The girls are disgusted by the whole thing and keep clear of the confrontations between the gangs, though a couple of them secretly admire Terry.

The two gangs engage in 'war games' from time to time, surging across the playground in fair imitation of a rugby rolling maul. But part of their code of conduct is that Terry and Jeff must never come into direct contact. They never speak to each other; never look directly at each other.

They often speak *about* each other. Sometimes the two gangs congregate at opposite ends of the playground, huddled around their respective leaders, mesmerised by the bully-boy rhetoric.

'If he doesn't stop using the soccer pitch when we want it, we'll get him—him and all the snivelling scumbags who hang around with him. I hate him. I hate all of them, especially those fucking Lebs and towel-heads,' says Terry, up one end, aping his dad.

'Nobody's going to push us around. After school, the pitch is ours—we were there first and we're going to keep it for as long as we like,' says Jeff, up the other end. 'Yeah,' say his mates.

'Except on Thursdays, when the girls use it for hockey,' says one of the neutrals, *sotto voce*, sitting on a nearby bench with his friends, trying not to laugh too much in case they attract any attention.

'Why doesn't Terry use it on Mondays and Wednesdays, and Jeff on Tuesdays and Fridays?' asks another, mainly for something to say.

Terry is shouting: 'Matter of fact, we're going to play soccer this afternoon, straight after school. Just let them try and stop us. I *hate* them.'

There's a roar of approval from the gang and they start to disperse as a teacher comes towards them and the bell rings to signal the end of lunch-time.

Down the other end, Jeff isn't quite finished. 'It's not just the soccer pitch. It's everything. Terry and his mob are bad, bad, bad. They're *evil*. They *smell*. They *stink*. Stinking, fucking Anglo arseholes—think they're better than everyone just 'cause they got here first. They'll go down. We're playing soccer this afternoon and any fucking afternoon we want to. We're better'n them. We can do whatever we want.'

Another roar. Boys cheering. Boys slapping each other on the back. Rude gestures made in the direction of the retreating members of Terry's gang.

No one is quite sure what happened next. Perhaps someone threw a stone; perhaps someone used a catapult, though their use was officially banned at school. Whatever the cause, and whichever side started it, the playground suddenly erupted into furious fighting. Punches were thrown; boys were being tackled, dragged along the ground and kicked. Someone produced a penknife and several boys received lacerations before the knife was lost in the melee. Several windows were broken by flying stones and a girl, running for cover, was hit in the face by a broken bottle that had been pulled out of a garbage bin and hurled into the air.

In the end, the playground looked like a battlefield with boys lying all over the asphalt, many bleeding and some sobbing—perhaps from pain, perhaps from shame. One was unconscious, a teacher bending over him and dabbing at a wound in his head.

An ambulance was called. Three boys were taken to hospital. One of them died an hour later, the result of a kick to the head.

His parents erected a discreet plaque on the wall of the school, near where their son had died. A solemn little ceremony was conducted during a school assembly, which gave the principal an opportunity to say a few words about hatred, revenge and the need for tolerance. Most eyes were fixed on the floor.

The soccer field was fenced and padlocked. No pupils were allowed to use it out of school hours.

The principal was transferred to an administrative job in the Department of Education. Jeff's parents sent him to a private school.

Is there anything more paradoxical than war?

Some of the finest citizens of every nation have distinguished themselves on the field of battle and become heroes to us all. They have been decorated for courage, for bravery or for their humanitarian work in raising the morale of their comrades in prisoner-of-war camps. People who might never have come to the attention of their communities have been thrust by war into the national consciousness. They are recalled with pride and gratitude.

Military bands play at festive occasions and stir our blood. Troops parading through the streets of our cities bring lumps to our throats and fill our eyes with tears of patriotism and pride.

Australia's most solemn day of reflection and most significant day of national celebration is Anzac Day, and its support is growing. On Anzac Day, people recall the heroism and sacrifice of those who have been prepared to fight and die for liberty, justice and the way of life we hold dear.

Some older people who recall their own privations as children growing up in the shadow of war look at the attitudes and behaviour of today's young people and say, 'What they need is a good war,' by which they presumably mean that times of war tend to bring out the best in civilian populations by giving people a focused sense of purpose.

Many people are excited by the prospect of war: it is not unusual for people to confess to 'thoroughly enjoying' modern media coverage of war. Some politicians show signs of enjoying their countries' involvement in wars that do not encroach on their homeland. The former UK Prime Minister Margaret Thatcher, referring to the Falklands Islands war, told a Scottish Conservative Party conference that 'it is exciting to have a real crisis on your hands, when you have spent half your political life dealing with humdrum issues like the environment'. (Yes, she really said that.)

From Abraham Lincoln's Gettysburg Address to the World War II broadcasts of Winston Churchill, national leaders produce some of their finest rhetoric when they address their citizens at ceremonies of remembrance, occasions for farewelling and welcoming troops, national crises, declarations of war and announcements of peace.

Across the nations of the world, some of the grandest and most moving structures have been created out of the experience of war: monuments to the fallen, memorials, fine statues and gardens laid out in memory of those who gave their lives in war.

People who have served in wars together experience a bond like no other—a lifelong sense of comradeship.

In the reserve units of a nation's armed forces, citizens willingly devote many hours of their spare time to military training and are praised for doing so.

In military academies, some of a nation's finest minds train some of its best and brightest young people.

Many of the greatest thinkers through history have praised war as a just remedy for wrongs done by countries that have failed to respect the sovereign rights of others. On all sides, religious leaders have spoken with confidence of God being on 'our' side. Politicians have unhesitatingly asserted that only a strong military force can ensure peace.

Here's what some of them have said:

Konrad Adenauer: 'An infallible method of conciliating a tiger is to allow oneself to be devoured.'

Winston Churchill: 'There are many things worse than war. Slavery is worse than war. Dishonour is worse than war.'

Billy Graham: 'We must have military power to keep madmen from taking over the world.'

Mao Zedong: 'Every Communist must grasp the truth: Political power grows out of the barrel of a gun.'

Margaret Thatcher: 'We have to see that the spirit of the South Atlantic—the real spirit of Britain—is kindled not only by war but can now be fired by peace. We have the first prerequisite. We know that we can do it—we haven't lost the ability [to win a war]. That is the Falklands Factor.'

George Washington: 'To be prepared for war is one of the most effectual means of preserving peace.'

On the other hand . . .

Those bright young men and women we have selected so carefully and trained so professionally are being prepared, in the final analysis, to be killers—though we prefer the noble term 'warriors'. We talk about 'defence forces', but acknowledge that 'the best form of defence is attack' (leading to the modern American doctrine of the pre-emptive strike, as practised in Iraq). We train our soldiers to drill perfectly so they will be conditioned to give absolute obedience to a superior officer who orders them to do things that, in normal circumstances, they would want to think twice about doing. At the moment of crisis, there won't be time to think twice. Their obedience training must be relentless if they are to kill on demand, without giving any thought to the possibility that the people they are killing are bright young people just like them, carefully selected and trained like them, probably apolitical like them, and now facing death when their potential as human beings has scarcely been realised. As Francis Bacon said, 'in peace the sons bury their fathers and in war the fathers bury their sons'. (Why don't the world's armies agree to a strict minimum age of, say, sixty for people sent into combat? That would put an old cat among the old pigeons.)

The 'glory' of war makes no sense to people who've been there. War is about blood and mud, broken limbs and shattered minds, brains and guts blown out of bodies and left for rats and scavenging birds to clean up. War is about lives forever changed by the horror of seeing, feeling, smelling and tasting violent death all around you. War is about aircrew being shot out of the sky, helicopters crashing into each other, soldiers being trapped and slaughtered inside their tanks, artillery fire catching its own forces unawares; it's about sailors being bombed and burned in ships and submarines, sinking to the ocean's floor in coffins of twisted steel.

Yes, it's getting 'cleaner' and more 'surgical' these days, with bombers flying high above their targets and computer-controlled weapons being launched by people sitting in clinically efficient, air-conditioned command posts. But it's neither clean nor surgical on the receiving end, and, in any case, someone eventually has to seize the enemy's territory and fight, up close, those who are defending it.

War is also, increasingly, about an assault on the planet. From the massive defoliation of Vietnam to the threat of nuclear fallout, we declare war not only on our enemies, but on our fragile ecology. War has always been about destruction, 'scorched earth', rubble, decimation and desolation, but new weapons apparently being planned by the US—such as those capable of being dropped from space or launched from 'hypersonic cruise vehicles'—put the whole world at risk.

We try to glorify war by the respect we pay those who have fought on our behalf, but they, more than anyone, know the truth: war is hell. It is hell for those who serve in the armed forces, who are at least trained for it; but what about the hell to which we consign civilian populations who find themselves, quite literally, caught in the crossfire and written off in the ledgers of modern warfare as 'collateral damage'? (In the case of all-out war, of course, civilians aren't collateral damage at all: they *are* the target. Just ask the survivors of bombing raids on cities like London, Berlin, Dresden, Hiroshima and Nagasaki, or the residents of cities recently identified as possible targets for North Korean missiles.)

Historians know another truth about war: it solves nothing, long-term. There is no 'war to end war'; old enemies become friends, allies become estranged, new enemies appear; territories are carved up; post-war arrangements come unstuck; and we go through it all again. Winners sometimes suffer and losers sometimes prosper, and sometimes it's the other way around. The sense of futility is never far from the moment of victory.

Families never recover from the loss of their loved ones in war. War is possibly the worst way to lose a son or daughter, a husband or wife, a friend or lover, because deaths in war—horrible, premature deaths—are part of the carefully calculated price willingly paid by the politicians who send their citizens to fight on their behalf . . . which is why we have to dress the whole miserable, disgusting enterprise in the dignified trappings of grand patriotism. How else could any of us cope?

Though many people behave virtuously within the appalling circumstances of a war—treating their prisoners with respect, showing compassion towards civilians, observing all the international conventions of 'civilised' war—no one could ever describe war itself as virtuous. At best, we could only ever call it the lesser of two evils: it was better to fight than to collude with an enemy; better to fight than be violated; better to fight than see a weak or helpless ally overwhelmed by force. Only ever 'better than'; never 'good'.

But if never 'good', what about 'just'? St Thomas Aquinas (1225–74) famously declared: 'For a war to be just, three conditions are necessary—public authority, just cause, right motive.' And, emboldened by that list, warriors and politicians have been talking about 'just' wars ever since. (Which leader ever admitted to embarking on an 'unjust' war?)

Here are the views of some people who have been either against war, or deeply sceptical about its value:

Ernest Bevin: 'There never has been a war yet which, if the facts had been put calmly before the ordinary folk, could not have been prevented . . . The common man, I think, is the great protection against war.'

Umberto Eco: 'War cannot be justified, because—in terms of the rights of the species—it is worse than a crime. It is a waste.'

Albert Einstein: 'How vile and despicable war seems to me! I would rather be hacked to pieces than take part in such an abominable business.'

Havelock Ellis: 'There is nothing that war has ever achieved we could not better achieve without it.'

Benjamin Franklin: 'There never was a good war, or a bad peace.'

Pope John XXIII: 'It is becoming humanly impossible to regard war, in this atomic age, as a suitable means of re-establishing justice when some right has been violated.'

Lyndon B. Johnson: 'In modern warfare, there are no victors; there are only survivors.'

John F. Kennedy: 'Mankind must put an end to war or war will put an end to mankind.'

Henry Kissinger: 'Henceforth, the adequacy of any military establishment will be tested by its ability to preserve the peace.'

Two new kinds of war

During the second half of the twentieth century, we witnessed a radically new kind of war—the 'Cold War', described by Umberto Eco as 'an *excellent* alternative to war . . . a humane and mild solution'. It is true that throughout most of the Cold War, the world was in a state of perpetual tension (and there were, in any case, some regional shooting wars as well—notably in Korea and Vietnam). Yet by comparison with the horrors of a major armed conflict, Eco is right: the Cold War was a remarkably effective way of dealing with international enmities without the mass slaughter that would inevitably have followed the outbreak of 'hot' war between the United States and the Soviet Union, especially if nuclear weapons had been deployed.

Just like the real thing, the Cold War produced some brilliant literature and cinema, some fine rhetoric, and it even produced a temporary winner—the US—following the collapse of communism in the Soviet Union and the apparent triumph of capitalism in the West.

It depended on two superpowers being in permanent stand-off, rattling their sabres at each other from time to time, arguing vociferously in meetings of the United Nations Security Council, forming alliances among the less powerful nations, and building frighteningly large arsenals of weapons—including the infamous intercontinental ballistic missiles. But all the roaring and threatening, all the fist thumping and strategic positioning of armies and navies, all the racing to be first in space, all the glaring and sulking amounted to a kind of *danse macabre* whose steps were as measured as any gavotte.

Like a couple of young teenagers allowed to go so far and no further, for whom penetrative sex was both endlessly fascinating and unthinkable, the superpowers tip-toed around the idea of 'mutually assured destruction'. The rest of the world watched their aggressive feinting, heard their calculations of the likely outcome of a nuclear strike and counter-strike, and wondered if it would ever happen. There were those who said it was the very existence of nuclear weapons too dreadful to unleash that would save the world from a nuclear holocaust. There were those who said the very opposite: the fact that such weapons had been manufactured would ensure they would one day be used.

But they weren't. Gradually the world's nervousness eased and the threat finally passed. Miraculously, the Soviet Union had broken up, and Russia and America were once again talking like potential allies.

Since the end of the Cold War, things have changed—and not for the better. Now we have yet another new form of war. Triggered by the terrorist attacks on the World

Trade Centre and the Pentagon on 11 September 2001 (via hijacked aircraft flying into those buildings), President George W. Bush pledged that the US and its allies would wage a 'war on terror'.

The rhetoric was clever: it sounded like a decisive response to the attacks on New York and Washington, but it created a new *category* of warfare that would allow the US to by-pass some of the old rules of the game. It also sounded rather like the 'war on poverty' or the 'war on drugs'—as though this were hardly a military matter at all.

The first expression of the war on terror was the US-led invasion of Afghanistan, in pursuit of the mastermind of the Al-Qaeda terrorist network, Osama bin Laden, thought to have been responsible for the terrorist attacks on the US.

The complexities of the war on terror quickly became evident. President Bush was forced on several occasions to make it clear that this was not a religious war—not a war on Islam—though many commentators described it as being exactly that, especially as the terrorists involved in the '9/11' attack were identified as Muslims, and messages were pouring out of the Islamic world condemning the US for its pro-Israel policies in the Middle East.

In Afghanistan, the ruling Taliban were accused of harbouring bin Laden, so the purpose of the invasion spread beyond a hunt for one man into a push for regime change. The Taliban were duly driven from power, but bin Laden was nowhere to be seen. (He was subsequently located and killed in Pakistan.) At the time of writing, it appeared that the

Taliban were re-emerging as a force in Afghanistan, filling the power vacuum between the various warring factions that temporarily replaced the Taliban as rulers of Afghanistan. *C'est la guerre.*)

The second expression of the war on terror was the invasion of Iraq. As in the case of Afghanistan, it looked remarkably like a conventional war ('if it quacks like a duck . . . '), though the goal was again said to be neither territorial nor religious. Although there were no apparent links between Iraq and the attacks of September 11, and although Saddam Hussein was widely regarded as being an enemy of Osama bin Laden and his Al-Qaeda network, Iraq was accused of having so-called 'weapons of mass destruction' that could be passed on to terrorist organisations. Like Afghanistan, the invasion of Iraq was also focused on the hunt for one man: Saddam Hussein.

Immediately following the invasion, when neither weapons nor Saddam could be found, the invasion was re-characterised as having been about the liberation of the Iraqi people from the yoke of Saddam's regime. To many people, this seemed only tenuously linked to the war on terror, especially as doubts emerged about the veracity of intelligence reports that had suggested Iraq was developing a nuclear weapons program. Writing in the *London Review of Books* about the British reaction to all this, John Lanchester pointed out that 'a large part of the population . . . want to know why we went to war, and want the reasons for it to have been satisfactorily explained in advance, rather than dredged up afterwards'.

Several moral issues arise from this new category of warfare.

If we describe a war in terms of such euphemisms as 'regime change' or 'pre-emptive strike', does this deny our opponents the legal protection and legitimacy traditionally given to the enemy? If the 'war on terror' is to be fought within a different moral framework from traditional warfare, does this mean the Geneva Conventions do not apply? Does it mean, for example, that prisoners taken during the invasion of Afghanistan were not to be regarded as prisoners of war in the traditional sense, and therefore not subject to international conventions regarding the treatment of prisoners? (US treatment of prisoners captured in Afghanistan and held without trial in Guantanamo Bay suggests it does.) Might this not mean, in turn, that soldiers involved in the invasion of Iraq (loosely connected, at least by political rhetoric, to the war on terror) might become confused about whether their prisoners were conventional prisoners of war, subject to the Geneva Conventions, or prisoners of the 'war on terror' with the quite different status implied by that? (Such confusion could perhaps help to explain the abuse by US military personnel of Iraqis held in the Abu Ghraib prison in Baghdad.)

Does any militarily powerful nation have the right to effect 'regime change' in cases where it doesn't approve of the behaviour of the government of another country? Is the 'pre-emptive strike' (the Bush doctrine, as applied in Iraq) morally different from any other form of aggression? If it is morally acceptable for the US to continue developing weapons of mass destruction, what moral objection can be raised against any other country choosing to do the same? Does the 'war on terror' give the US and its allies freedom to be militarily pro-active without needing to declare war, in the conventional sense, on the countries they invade? What is the moral distinction between an invasion mounted in the name of 'war on terror' and any other kind of invasion? Since this new kind of war is supposed to be focused on the pursuit and apprehension of individual terrorists who have committed crimes, is it a proper task for armed services, or should it be left to the intelligence and police services of the countries in which those crimes were committed?

Or, as the veteran Washington journalist Helen Thomas enquired of the press secretary to President Bush: 'Why would we kill thousands of innocent Iraqis to take out one man?'

The new voice of pacifism

The end of the Cold War offered some hope that old-style shooting wars, at least on a large scale, might be a thing of the past. The Cold War had shown that things could be handled differently—not ideally, but at least differently. But the war on terror appears to have changed the rules of engagement, leaving many people confused about an acceptable moral framework for going to war.

In response, a new breed of pacifist has appeared. Traditional pacifism is opposed to all forms of violence and will not countenance warfare under any conditions. Most people do not embrace that hard-line version of pacifism, partly because, as André Comte-Sponville puts it in his discussion of gentleness, 'to espouse pacifism is to make of gentleness a system or an absolute and to deny oneself the possibility of effectively defending, at least in certain circumstances, the very thing one claims as a principle—namely, peace'. Comte-Sponville therefore distinguishes between the *pacifists,* who oppose war utterly, and the *peaceable,* who are prepared to defend peace even with the use of force. Simone Weil made the case for peaceability in *Gravity and Grace*:

> Non-violence is no good unless it is effective. [In relation to a young man's question to Ghandi about defending his sister], the answer should have been: use force unless you are such that you can defend her with as much chance of success without violence . . . We should strive to become such that we are able to be non-violent.

The new voice of pacifism is not quite the same as the old, and not quite the same as being merely peaceable. Perhaps influenced by the Cold War and its peaceful resolution, the new pacifists refuse to return to pre-Cold War attitudes and values. They are fed up with war; they believe it is outmoded; they plead for a more civilised and grown-up approach to conflict resolution. They have come to associate war with the primitive brutality of the savage, or the immaturity of the school bully. They acknowledge that the warrior mentality, like the hunter mentality, is buried deep in the masculine psyche (many, perhaps most, new pacifists seem to be women), but they think it's time to confine the expression of that urge to the sporting field or perhaps the cut-throat world of commercial competition—not the battlefield.

The new pacifists yearn for a radical shift in our thinking, to the point where we reject war as an option, not only because it is an obscenity, but also because it has proved to be so futile in practice. They can scarcely believe that at this stage of our social evolution, we are still prepared to pick up a gun to settle a dispute; still prepared to invade another country to make a point; still training people to fight instead of negotiate.

Even when it comes to defending ourselves against the threat of aggression, the new pacifists believe that diplomacy can work, as it does when spouses, neighbours or corporations settle a dispute—in court or out of it. Resolutions aren't always entirely satisfactory to both parties because compromises will usually be called for, but new pacifists think such compromises, at an international level, should *always* be preferred to the mass violence, terror, destruction and despair wrought by war.

New pacifists are in favour of open and continuous dialogue. When North Korea was making aggressive noises about its nuclear weapons program in mid-2003 and various leaders of other countries were meeting in crisis talks with each other, the new pacifists shook their heads in bewilderment:

'Why aren't all these politicians talking *to* Kim Jong-Il, the North Korean leader, instead of talking to each other *about* him?' In 2018, when Kim Jong-Il's successor, Kim Jong-Un, was making similar threats, US president Donald Trump did indeed arrange a face-to-face meeting with him, as he subsequently also did with Russian president Vladimir Putin. In spite of a significant build-up of US military strength, the Trump doctrine appeared to focus on economic rather than military warfare with trade sanctions the chief weapon. (At the time of writing, it was not clear whether this would make Trump a hero of the new pacifists, especially as he seemed intent on fomenting enmity between the US and its traditional allies.)

The suspicion in the minds of many people is that leaders are generally reluctant to talk directly to their potential enemies because they are actually drawn to the idea of going to war or, at least, because they want to keep that option alive, since incumbent governments tend to strengthen their electoral position when they are involved in a war well away from their homeland. (Face-to-face contact also carries the risk of easing the tension in the relationship and making belligerent rhetoric—'sabre-rattling'—appear ridiculous.)

Umberto Eco speaks for the new breed in his 1991 essay 'Reflections on War' when he calls for a *taboo* on war. Acknowledging that a taboo can't normally be proclaimed but must grow spontaneously and organically out of our experience, Eco believes the time required for such organic growth is shortening. He asserts that 'It is an intellectual duty to proclaim the inconceivability of war.'

History has not been kind to such grand ideas: the Kellogg–Briand Pact of 1928, outlawing war, was signed by virtually all members of the ill-fated League of Nations, but had no discernible impact on the bellicosity of those who stood to benefit—politically or financially—from war. Perhaps Eco's idea might yet find its time: after all, it was once generally accepted that slavery was an inherent, inevitable feature of human society, and capital punishment was once almost universally regarded as 'natural', both as a legitimate form of revenge and as a deterrent. In both cases it took strong moral leadership, rather than mere 'organic growth', to bring about change. Is it too much to hope that, one day, we will be inspired to regard war as being as absurd, as obscene and as inconceivable as we would now regard slavery, or as abhorrent as capital punishment now seems in civilised societies?

How much can we decide for ourselves?

'Should we ever go to war?' might seem to have been a strange chapter to include in a book about the art of making *personal* moral choices. After all, the decision to wage war is the biggest a nation can make, and individuals—especially those opposed to war—often feel powerless in the face of it.

Yes, you can be a conscientious objector, and the emerging attitudes of young people around the world suggest that the ranks of passive resistors and conscientious objectors might be swelling as we move into the twenty-first century against the background of the twentieth century's appalling record as the 'century of war'. (Many people dare to harbour the hope that the twenty-first century, by contrast, will come to be known as 'the century of healing', though the early signs aren't encouraging.)

But not all peace-lovers are pacifists. Many of us would be prepared to play our part in a war if, in the end, there were no alternative and if our role were clearly that of defender rather than aggressor. Yet we would first want to do all we could to avert such a calamity.

Even if we were to concede, grudgingly, the probability that war will never be entirely eradicated, those who see war as a futile vestige of a more primitive era should never give up trying to influence the course of events. We must ensure that our elected representatives know how we feel. As citizens, we have one voice each, and a perfect right to have it heard. If we believe them, we should say these things loudly and often:

- We regard war as an outmoded and fundamentally flawed strategy for conflict resolution.
- We acknowledge the need to fight, as a last resort, in defence of our freedom and in support of our allies, but we claim no moral right to interfere in the regimes of other countries by force.
- We expect those who represent us in international diplomacy to exhaust every conceivable avenue of

negotiation—including constant face-to-face contact with their alleged enemies—before daring to take such a retrograde step as declaring war on another nation.

At an even more personal level, there are two practical moral lessons to be drawn from discussion of this most distressing of all human phenomena. First, if we seriously aspire to eliminate war from the repertoire of human possibilities, we must begin by ensuring that the values that give rise to war are not being promoted in our own homes, nor practised in our communities and workplaces. One small step towards the ultimate elimination of war is the active promotion of *personal* peace and harmony, and the elimination of prejudice, hatred and violence in our own lives and within our own circle. If we believe consultation and negotiation are better strategies than violent conflict, we'd better be prepared to consult and negotiate.

Second, those who are plunged into morally repugnant situations created by war can still choose to act with integrity. In whatever circumstances we may find ourselves, it is appropriate to ask: 'What is the right thing for me to do now?' This won't necessarily lead us to act non-violently, but it will encourage us to act in ways likely to produce the best possible outcome for all concerned, given the conditions under which we are operating. The real heroes of resistance movements, prisoner-of-war camps, or even of actual combat, have always been those who made good moral choices in bad circumstances.

William Temple (1881–1944), when he was Archbishop of Canterbury, said of England's participation in World War II: 'We are called to the hardest of all tasks; to fight without hatred, to resist without bitterness, and, in the end, if God grant it so, to triumph without vindictiveness.'

18

Does biotechnology pose new ethical problems?

The short answer to that question is 'no'. While it is obvious that biotechnology is one of the newest and most exciting frontiers of science, and the ethical issues raised by such developments as embryonic stem cell research and human cloning have never been raised in these particular contexts before, the issues themselves are not new.

The moral approach to any of them is the same as the approach to abortion, contraception, in-vitro fertilisation (IVF), organ transplants . . . or the use of human beings for medical research. In every case we have to ask ourselves the same old questions: Is this action in harmony with my concept of virtue? Is it consistent with my sense of personal integrity? Do I believe that what I am proposing involves an appropriate recognition of the rights, needs and wellbeing of others? Is self-interest blinding me to the moral issues? Will anyone be harmed by this and, if so, am I falling for the trap of thinking that the end justifies the means?

One of the special features of the rapidly developing science of biotechnology is that it draws us into a debate about the nature of life itself. As in the abortion debate, tricky technical questions arise: When can a foetus be said to be a person? What is the moral status of a frozen human embryo, stored for the purposes of research? Who 'owns' such embryos? Can their destruction be regarded as the destruction of life? What are the moral rights of surrogate mothers who agree to carry an implanted foetus to term, give birth, and then hand the child to its 'biological' parents?

As with most complex ethical questions, thoughtful people of goodwill disagree over particular cases: there are no blanket principles that point us to the universal right answer to every ethical question raised by biotechnology, medicine, psychology or any other field of scientific endeavour. Each scientist, in a spirit of moral mindfulness, must find the right answers in each set of circumstances.

For example, embryonic stem cell research was once the subject of vigorous moral debate, particularly when it emerged that embryos would die in the process of having their stem cells removed.

The embryos in question were surplus to the IVF program—that is, they were created by in-vitro fertilisation in numbers too great to be required by the program. Opponents of the research program argued that these surplus embryos should be destroyed outright, rather than used for research. Politicians, theologians, journalists—as well as biologists and stem cell researchers themselves—were caught up in the debate. Some argued that this was yet another step in the process of diminishing the special status of human life: that it abandoned the principle that human life should never be used as a means to an end; that a decision to proceed with embryonic stem cell research would open the door to even more alarming developments in biotechnology that could not yet be imagined.

Others could find no significant moral difference between destroying the embryos as a consequence of removing their stem cells, and destroying them outright. Still others argued, more pragmatically, that the potential benefits of stem cell research far outweighed any moral queasiness about the fate of the embryos.

That debate was an interesting demonstration of the fact that the arguments were timeless; only the content was new. Was the essential argument in favour that 'the end justifies the means', or was it that there is nothing *inherently* wrong with the use of human embryos for medical research? Why did the researchers in question think it was such a straightforward matter: were they proposing, as some had grimly hinted, the latest in a line of dubious scientific experiments running back to Nazi Germany's notorious human experimenter Dr Mengele, or had their familiarity with the embryonic material convinced them there was no moral issue at all? Would the moral debate have been different if the embryos had been specially created for the purposes of medical research, rather than merely being surplus 'stock' from the IVF program?

The reason why the debate about embryonic stem cell research became so heated was presumably because it was raising questions about the value we should attach to human life in any form, and about potential exploitation of the reproductive process. Dark images were evoked: sexual activity being, in the future, purely for the expression of love and/or lust, utterly detached from procreation; babies being created in scientific 'farms' where rows of frozen embryos would await their parents' convenience; terminally ill people being 'volunteered' for medical research; human life being so little respected that we would plunder the bodies of 'useless' people for spare parts to implant into the bodies of worthier recipients—a heart-diseased genius, for instance, being entitled to receive the healthy heart of an idiot or a layabout.

Did anyone seriously imagine that using unwanted, non-sentient embryos for medical research, rather than destroying them, would put us on the slippery slope towards any of that? (We were not, after all, proposing to slit the throats of toddlers.)

If you had been utterly opposed to researchers' use of stem cells from human embryos, the toughest of all your moral dilemmas might turn out to be this one: suppose your child suffered from a debilitating disease like transverse myelitis, or you yourself had Parkinson's disease or motor neurone disease. Would you decline treatment arising from medical research that had used embryonic cells, even if you were satisfied that no pain or distress had been caused to anyone in the process?

Generally speaking, science does whatever can be done: the natural tendency of the scientific community is to attempt whatever seems possible, even if only out of scientific curiosity. The rest of us assume—or perhaps we merely hope—that the vast majority of scientists want to make a positive contribution to the well-being of the human species. But we sometimes wonder: if we were to hand over the moral responsibility for all bio-medical research to scientists, could we be sure they would be as interested in the moral questions as the scientific questions?

Here is how Dr Francis Collins, the co-ordinator of the International Human Genome Project, puts it:

> Scientists alone cannot—and should not—make major societal decisions about the proper uses of these new and powerful technologies. The human genome, and the responsibility for its benevolent application, belongs to all of humanity.

Questions about moral aspects of biotechnology raise broader questions about the training of scientists and our ever-increasing tendency to separate the sciences from the humanities. This is far from being a new issue: in 1959, the British scientist, civil servant and acclaimed novelist, C.P. Snow (1905–80), delivered the Rede Lecture on 'The Two Cultures and the Scientific Revolution'. Snow argued that society was leaving moral questions about science (especially, at that time, nuclear science) to scientists who had grown up in a sub-culture where such questions were either not raised at all or inadequately explored. He was equally concerned about the reverse problem: although people trained in the humanities, including philosophy and literature, might be equipped to make useful contributions to any discussion of moral questions, they were (and still are) being educated within an intellectual sub-culture where science was rarely discussed, little understood, and sometimes openly despised.

Moral mindfulness is as important for scientists as for anyone. Our nervousness about the decisions they might make is based on the perfectly legitimate fear that they might not be equipped to recognise the moral dimensions of some of the opportunities they encounter on the frontiers of science.

The solution to concerns about biotechnology is unlikely to be found in tougher legislation, but in a radically different approach to the blending of science and the humanities in our education system—especially at the tertiary level. At present, we seem to be travelling in precisely the opposite direction from the one most likely to produce that outcome.

Looking to the future, it is perfectly possible that developments in biotechnology undreamed of at present will transform the way we reproduce, raise our children, deal with disease and even, perhaps, choose when we will die. All such possibilities will be, of themselves, morally neutral until we decide to implement them: then we shall have to decide, case by case, whether they can be justified on moral grounds.

Many people once thought that any form of contraception was so contrary to nature as to be morally wrong. Some still do. (Go back far enough, though, and people had no idea there was a causal link between sex and pregnancy.) When we heard the news in 1978 that the world's first 'test-tube baby' had been born, many people were alarmed to discover it was possible to manage a conception by joining sperm to eggs in a vitreous dish and wondered at its moral implications: could this process be abused in some way? There was talk then—as there is today when the subject of human cloning is raised—that this was the work of the devil, the newborn baby was 'Frankenstein's child' and scientists were 'playing God'. By the time the first IVF baby, Louise Brown, celebrated her 40th birthday (on 25 July 2018), about eight million babies had been conceived *in vitro*. IVF is no longer the subject of popular moral debate: it is generally recognised as a welcome option for the small minority of people who cannot conceive naturally and who so desperately want a child that they are prepared to subject themselves to the disciplines and expense of the process.

The focus of concern in the field of human reproduction has shifted to cloning, and all the things once said about IVF are being said again about the prospect of human babies being produced through biotechnology that challenges our conventional idea of conception. One of the two British scientists who oversaw the artificial conception of Louise Brown, Professor Robert Edwards, has given qualified encouragement to Dr Severino Antinori, the Italian researcher in charge of a human cloning research program, by suggesting that he wouldn't object in principle to the cloning of a child, 'provided all the embryos after cloning are as normal as those after normal conception. [Antinori] can't say that at the moment. No one can.'

No doubt a human cloning project will ultimately succeed; no doubt it will be controversial; no doubt a tiny group of people will, for various reasons, want to take advantage of it; no doubt the overwhelming majority of couples will choose to conceive their babies in the traditional, sexual way. The choice will be for each of them to make.

The science of organ transplants sparked moral outrage when it began: the first transplantation of a human heart by South Africa's Dr Christian Barnard stimulated worldwide debate and provoked the British journalist Malcolm Muggeridge to ask Dr Barnard, in a televised forum, whether he thought it significant that this operation was first carried out 'in a country that places so little value on human life'—a question that sparked its own moral outrage. Today, the transplantation of various organs—especially kidneys—is generally regarded as being no more controversial than a blood transfusion. Heart transplants and the implantation of artificial hearts are somewhat more newsworthy—perhaps because the operation is more complicated, the risk of failure greater and the symbolism more dramatic.

Almost everything that science offers us can be used beneficially, yet almost every scientific advance can also be abused. When it comes to the moral question—in biotechnology as in personal relationships, business, sport or war—we must each decide for ourselves. But this is not the same as saying we should simply please ourselves: if we are engaged in the serious pursuit of 'goodness', the habit of moral mindfulness will get us there. Over and over again, we must ask ourselves *Is this right?* And then, in a spirit of compassion and sensitivity to the well-being of everyone involved in the issue, we must listen carefully to our own answer.

The wrap

Freedom to choose is no freedom at all unless it is accompanied by the confidence of knowing we have made the *right* choice.

●

Moral decision-making is a subjective process, but that doesn't mean 'anything goes'. Although there might be no absolute rules to guide my every decision—no universal 'right answers'—there is always a right answer for me, here and now, and it is my personal responsibility to work out what it is.

●

The right answer for me may be different from the right answer for you, and the right answer for me in my present circumstances may be different from the right answer for me in another set of circumstances.

•

Moral certainty is not always available to us: we must sometimes choose between alternatives that are neither obviously
right nor obviously wrong.

•

Utilitarians believe that any action intended to promote
wellbeing and prevent suffering (or, more simplistically, to
maximise pleasure and minimise pain) is 'right' and any action
that increases suffering or diminishes wellbeing (or produces
more pain than pleasure) is 'wrong'. The problem lies in
knowing what actions will maximise pleasure and minimise
pain *for all concerned*.

•

The moral sense is a social sense. Personal relationships are
both the wellspring and the lifeblood of morality. Our moral
sensitivity is heightened when we feel connected with the
communities in which we exist (at home, in the neighbourhood, at school, at work). When communities fragment,
shared values are the first casualty.

•

Morality is different from law. The law is about dispensing
justice; morality is about fairness. The law is about obedience;

morality is about choice. You can be legally right but morally wrong.

●

The ethical frameworks of most Western countries are described as Judeo-Christian, as a way of acknowledging their religious origins. Yet moral development often takes place outside any religious framework, and religion does its most positive *moral* work when it promotes the idea of compassion—charity, kindness, respect, forgiveness—rather than offering dogmatic moral prescriptions. At its best, religion reinforces the noblest human ideals and values; at its worst, it stifles open enquiry and foments judgmental moralising.

●

Rewards and punishments confuse our sense of right and wrong. We ought to do the right thing because it is right, not because we will be rewarded for doing it. If we offer rewards to children for doing the right thing, they will learn to seek rewards: doing the right thing will become a means to an end rather than an end in itself.

●

Being morally sensitive means taking other people seriously—not judging them for the moral choices they make, nor trying to change their minds by putting them under pressure. (You can't control other people, but you can control your own response to them.)

●

Deciding what's right and wrong is not only a matter of striving to maximise wellbeing and minimise suffering; it is also a matter of striving to behave virtuously—imagining an ideal standard of goodness to which we can aspire. '*Is it good?*' trumps '*Is it right?*'

●

Moral mindfulness is the pathway to moral clarity—a way of stoking the moral engine we call 'conscience'. It is a habit that can be acquired by constant practice of a threefold discipline: being fully aware, moment by moment, of the ethical dimension of whatever you are doing; pondering what you have learned from previous experience in similar situations; and imagining the likely consequences for all concerned.

●

We can stimulate our moral mindfulness by 'tests' such as the Rotary four-way test, the test of public exposure, the sniff test, the tell-the-children test . . . or perhaps a 'super-test' like this one: 'Would I do this if it were *the one and only action* by which other people were going to judge my integrity and write my epitaph?'

●

Morality is the work of the imagination: making moral choices is a creative act that, like all creative acts, requires courage and involves risk. When confronted by two possible courses of action, try to visualise them as two complete scenarios: cast yourself as the central character in both and then imagine how each story might unfold.

●

Guilt is an authentic human emotion that reassures us our moral machinery is in working order, but it must be dealt with properly. When it is nursed beyond its 'use by' date, it becomes corrosive. Guilt is usually a sign that we need to apologise to those we have wronged and seek their forgiveness.

●

Forgiveness is a liberating, healing experience for the forgiver and the forgiven. We can't will ourselves to 'forgive and forget', but we can forgive and then live as if we have truly forgiven. Forgiveness is not about forgetting; it's about moving on.

•

Every action undertaken on the way to achieving a morally acceptable goal should itself be morally acceptable. Even a worthy goal cannot be used to justify a morally dubious means of achieving it.

•

Sexual desire creates a moral minefield, but prurient and judgmental gossip about other people's sexual activities may be more damaging—and contribute more to the sum of human pain and unhappiness—than sexual misbehaviour.

•

The thing we most resent or criticise in others is often the thing we have refused to acknowledge as one of our own frailties.

•

Understanding and acceptance are morally preferable to mere tolerance. We don't need more *tolerance* of immigrants, 'ethnics', Muslims, Indigenous Australians, asylum-seekers or any other minority groups; what we need is more *curiosity*; more openness. We need to master the art of getting to know each other better.

•

Lying is occasionally justifiable, but lying that deceives in order to gain an advantage over another person is always wrong. The most damaging lies are those we tell ourselves.

•

The moral muteness of managers—failing to ask, constantly and habitually, *Is this right?*—creates an organisational climate in which management appears to be an amoral activity, economic considerations are paramount, and employees feel able to behave less ethically at work than in their personal lives.

•

People who are going to be affected by a decision have the right to be consulted before that decision is made.

•

The new breed of pacifist yearns for a paradigm shift in which we reject war as an option, not only because it is an obscenity, but also because it has proved to be so futile in practice. One small step towards the ultimate elimination of war from the repertoire of human possibilities is the active promotion of *personal* peace and the elimination of prejudice, hatred and violence from our own lives and within our own circle.

●

We are more likely to achieve peace of mind when we attend to the needs and well-being of others than when we single-mindedly pursue our own happiness.

●

Even when we share the same values and try to live in harmony with the same virtues, we won't always agree with each other about what's right and wrong in particular cases. But wise moral decisions will always acknowledge our inter-dependency: our moral choices are ours alone, but they bind us to all those who will be affected by them. So deciding *for yourself* what's right and wrong does not mean deciding *in isolation*. Though we may sometimes feel like independent little boats bobbing about on the surface of some trackless ocean, we are actually more like the strands of a vast, evolving web. We depend on our connections with each other for our sense of identity, morality, emotional security and psychological well-being; in that sense, we belong to each other.

Further reading

Simon Blackburn, *Being Good*, Oxford University Press, 2001

André Comte-Sponville, *A Short Treatise on the Great Virtues*, Vintage, 2003

Lama Surya Das, *Awakening the Buddha Within*, Bantam Books, 1997

Umberto Eco, *Five Moral Pieces*, Secker & Warburg, 2001

Stephen Law, *The Philosophy Gym*, Review, 2003

Iris Murdoch, *The Sovereignty of Good*, Routledge, 1971

Richard Noonan, *The Moral Philosophers*, Clarendon Press, 1983

Peter Singer, *Writings on an Ethical Life*, Fourth Estate, 2000

James Q. Wilson, *The Moral Sense*, The Free Press, 1993

Acknowledgments

This book was the idea of my publisher, Lisa Highton, who also offered inspiration and guidance on the several occasions when the project seemed beyond me. The title was suggested by David Dale. The editor of the first edition, Deonie Fiford, took a rough book and made it smoother.

The proposal for this substantially revised and updated third edition of *Right & Wrong* came from Fiona Hazard, Publishing Director at Hachette, and I am grateful to her for her strong support. I have also greatly benefitted from the perceptive and skilful guidance of my editor at Hachette, Rebecca Allen, who has played a significant role in helping me refresh my expression of the book's ideas and arguments.

I am grateful to Professor Christopher Beness for supplying me with the scientific data about spontaneous abortions mentioned in Chapter 16, and to Alanna Mackay for alerting me to the Kellogg–Briand Pact and its implications, mentioned in Chapter 17.

The development of the ideas in this book was stimulated by conversations over many years with wise and generous friends, colleagues and teachers. I want to express particular appreciation to Meg Hart, Bruce Kaye, Gina Kourt, Robert McLaughlin, Keith Mason, John Vallance and the late Meredith Ryan for their advice, encouragement and support.

Index